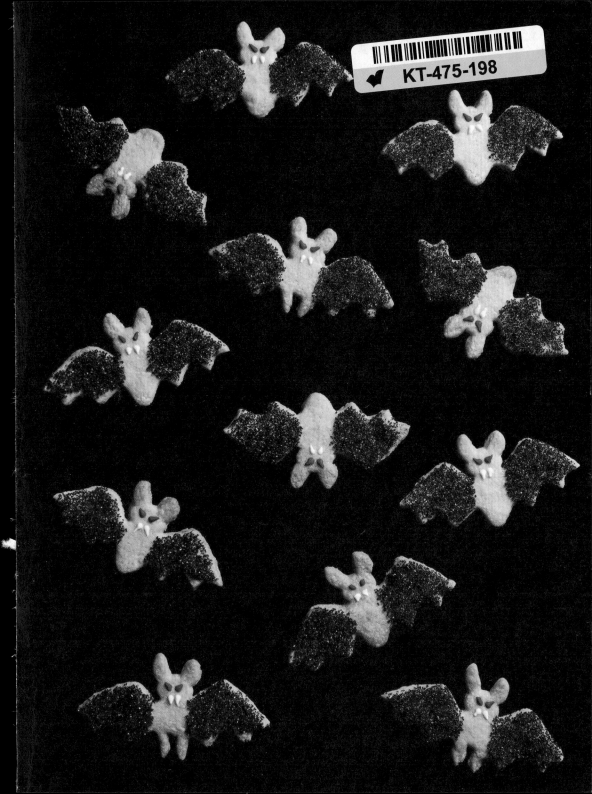

THE

WICKED

BAKER

THE WICKED BAKER

CAKES AND TREATS TO *die* FOR

Helena Garcia

Photography by Patricia Niven

Hardie Grant

QUADRILLE

Contents

Introduction

Welcome all to my wonderful world of creepy bakes and unusual desserts! I can't express enough how delighted I am to have been given the opportunity to put this little book together. Although many of you would want to use these bakes as inspiration for Halloween, the flavours and concepts are suitable all year round. I have spent hours in the kitchen developing delicious recipes as well as fun and bizarre projects. This means that if you feel like making a delightful chocolate-peanut butter cake, buttery cookies or a vegan dessert, you can refer to this book. You see Mr Hollywood, style and substance are in one place!

Since I was a teenager, I have been fascinated with all things strange and obscure. Learning that most of our festivals and celebrations come from pagan traditions opened a whole new world for me when I was younger. A world I felt connected to.

My grandparents come from Celtic Galicia in Spain, and it's the Celts we need to thank for creating my favourite celebration. Halloween is a holiday which brings me immense joy throughout the year. It is present in everything I do, how I dress, the way I decorate my house and, of course, my baking style.

I first experienced Halloween when I was 17. I spent my last year of high school in Las Vegas, USA. Throughout October the school was completely decorated, and everyone came to class in costume, including the teachers. The houses on the street I lived in had their garages open and were transformed into haunted houses. The stores were bursting with pumpkins, candy, skeletons and pointy hats. I was hooked.

My obsession evolved throughout the years and when I was given the opportunity to take over a Victorian-style apothecary in Leeds, cauldrons and potion bottles started appearing on its antique mahogany shelves.

My aim has always been to turn what was seen as a tacky and commercial holiday into a sophisticated and spiritual one. Ultimately, Halloween is European and it's time to bring it back home and reclaim it.

I tend to see beauty where others see darkness, but I find that if you apply a little touch of humour to macabre concepts, the result is an array of opportunity. I do tend to stay away from gory projects because, after all, I am creating delicious food. However, I know there are some real gore junkies out there, so I have sneaked in a brain cinnamon roll (page 72) just for you bloodthirsty folk.

I love cooking in general, but baking feels like cooking with added creative possibilities. Most of the baking projects in this book have a spooky decorative touch, but not all. There are recipes for all skill levels, from simple cookies to an elaborate four-layer haunted tree cake (page 27). I just hope these bakes bring you as much joy as creating them have brought me.

Cooking note: The recipes in this book were tested in a fan-assisted [convection] oven. If your oven is not fan-assisted, raise the Celsius temperatures given throughout by 20°C.

The Fahrenheit temperatures in the book are for regular (non-fan) ovens.

CAKES & CUPCAKES

Vampire Tears Candle Cake

SERVES 6-8

Sponge

285g [2 cups] plain [all-purpose] flour

1 tsp bicarbonate of soda [baking soda]

1 tsp salt

4 Tbsp cocoa powder

2½ Tbsp red food colour

1 tsp vanilla extract

115g [½ cup] unsalted butter, at room temperature

300g [1½ cups] caster [granulated] sugar

2 large eggs

240ml [1 cup] buttermilk

1 Tbsp white wine vinegar

Cream cheese frosting

225g [1 cup] full-fat cream cheese, at room temperature

55g [¼ cup] salted butter, at room temperature

360g [3 cups] icing [confectioners'] sugar

50g [½ cup] black or regular cocoa powder

black food colour

To decorate

340g [12oz] red Candy Melts

1–2 Tbsp vegetable oil

black birthday candles

These candle cakes are based on 'blood' candles I have at home. They're covered in black wax but when you light them, they drip red 'blood'. I think they're really cool, so I just had to adapt them into an edible equivalent. It is a straightforward recipe and perfect for a centrepiece dessert. The cake base is red velvet. A little tip to get a darker black buttercream: make it the day before as it darkens with time.

Preheat the oven to 160°C fan [350°F/Gas mark 4] and line a 23 x 33-cm [9 x 13-in] baking tray – the kind you would use for a Swiss [jelly] roll – with baking paper.

For the sponge, sift the flour, bicarbonate of soda and salt into a medium bowl and set aside.

In a smaller bowl, mix the cocoa powder, red food colour and vanilla extract to form a thick paste. Set aside.

Cream the butter and caster sugar together in an electric mixer until light and fluffy. Add the eggs, one by one, and continue mixing until fully incorporated.

Add the cocoa and food colour paste and mix, making sure to scrape down the sides and base of the bowl.

Add half the buttermilk and mix in, then add half the flour mixture and mix in, then repeat with the rest of the buttermilk and flour. Add the vinegar, then increase the speed to high and mix until everything is incorporated. Pour the batter into the prepared baking tray and bake for 25 minutes, or until a skewer stuck into the middle comes out clean.

Meanwhile, make the cream cheese frosting. Mix the cream cheese and butter together in an electric mixer until light and fluffy. Turn the speed to low and add the icing sugar, a little at a time. Add the cocoa powder and enough black food colour to get the right shade.

When the cake is ready and cool, level it with a serrated knife, then cut out 6 circles with a 10-cm [4-in] diameter cookie cutter.

Assemble the first candle by layering and icing the first 3 circles of cake. Smooth the frosting around the sides with a palette knife and insert a skewer in the centre to keep it stable. Repeat using 2 circles of cake to make a shorter candle, then use the final circle to make a candle that has been very burnt down. Don't smooth the tops as candles dip in the middle. Chill the assembled cakes in the fridge for 45 minutes.

Melt the Candy Melts according to the packet instructions or in the microwave at 30-second intervals, then mix in 1–2 Tbsp of vegetable oil to loosen it a little. Pour into a piping [pastry] bag and drip over the candles. Leave it to set, then repeat the process. The more times you repeat the process the fuller the 'wax' will look. Insert a birthday candle in the middle of each cake and light before serving.

* Photographed on previous spread

Poison Candy Apple Cake

SERVES 12-14

225ml [1 cup] vegetable oil, plus extra for oiling

400g [2 cups] granulated sugar

3 eggs

250g [2 cups] plain [all-purpose] flour

1 tsp baking powder

¼ tsp salt

3 Tbsp ground cinnamon

4 small apples, peeled, cored and chopped into small chunks

150g [1 cup] chopped walnuts

Icing
115g [½ cup] salted butter

220g [1 cup] dark brown sugar

60ml [¼ cup] whole milk

icing [confectioners'] sugar, sifted

To decorate
red fondant icing

piping gel or liquid glucose

125g [1 cup] peanuts, chopped

wooden stick

green leaf

This is such a fun project that, believe me, can be made by beginner bakers. There's a minimal amount of carving and the fondant icing doesn't need to be completely perfect. I'm using fresh apple to flavour this cake and the icing [frosting] is made by boiling milk, butter and sugar together. One bite and you'll be dead... from pure pleasure!

Preheat the oven to 170°C fan [375°F/Gas mark 5] and oil 2 x 15-cm [6-in] hemisphere cake tins and a 15-cm [6-in] round cake tin.

Mix the oil, granulated sugar and eggs together in an electric mixer on medium speed. Add the flour, baking powder, salt and cinnamon and continue mixing until it is fully incorporated.

Using a wooden spoon or spatula, gently stir in the fresh apple and chopped walnuts, then divide the batter between the prepared cake tins. Bake for 40–45 minutes until a skewer stuck into the middle comes out clean. Leave to cool in the tins for 5–10 minutes before turning out onto a wire rack.

For the icing [frosting], bring the butter and brown sugar to a simmer in a saucepan over a low-medium heat. Add the milk and bring to the boil. Remove from the heat and leave to cool slightly, then add enough icing sugar to make it thick enough to ice the cake.

After your cakes are baked, cooled and levelled, cut a small slice off the bottom of one semi-sphere and glue to your cake board or stand using a little bit of the icing. Spread the semi-sphere with icing and add the flat cake layer. Ice again and top it with the other semi-sphere, curved side up.

cont...

Carve a round hollow at the top for the stalk, using a real apple as reference. Spread a thin layer of icing over the whole cake and set aside.

On a surface dusted with icing sugar, roll out the red fondant icing to a 3mm [⅛in] thickness. Use to cover the cake and smooth out.

Brush the piping gel or glucose over the bottom half of the apple and cover with the chopped peanuts, using your hand to stick the peanuts in place.

Cover 5cm [2in] of your wooden stick in foil and insert into the hollow you've made on top of the apple cake. Finally, insert the leaf.

The Witch is in the Princess Cake!

MAKES 2 MINI CAKES

3 large eggs

150g [¾ cup] caster [granulated] sugar

1 Tbsp whole milk

120g [1 cup] plain [all-purpose] flour, sifted

¾ tsp baking powder

2 Tbsp raspberry jam

Custard
2 large egg yolks

40g [3¼ Tbsp] caster [granulated] sugar

1 Tbsp cornflour [cornstarch]

1 tsp vanilla bean paste

250ml [1 cup] whole milk

Mascarpone cream
240ml [1 cup] whipping cream

50g [½ cup] icing [confectioners'] sugar, sifted

180g [¾ cup] mascarpone cheese

1 Tbsp plus 1 tsp vanilla bean paste

To decorate
350g [12oz] marzipan or purple fondant icing

purple food colour (optional)

black edible paint or pen

This is my take on the fabulous and cheerful Swedish cake, prinsesstårta – layers of sponge, raspberry jam and mascarpone cream, topped with marzipan. The witch has been trapped in the cakes and only her legs are on show.

The day before making the cake, make the witch's legs. Take 2 pieces of marzipan, each the size of a golf ball, and tint them purple with food colour paste, or use purple fondant icing. Shape into large logs, cut in half to give you equal size legs, then shape the feet and knees. It helps to use a picture for reference. Leave them to harden overnight, then paint on the stripes with black edible paint or pen.

The next day, preheat the oven to 220°C [475°F/Gas mark 9] and line a baking tray – the kind you would use for a Swiss [jelly] roll – with baking paper.

In a stand mixer fitted with a whisk attachment, whisk the eggs and sugar together until pale and fluffy. Add the milk and mix again.

In a separate bowl, sift the flour and baking powder together. Add to the egg mixture, folding in carefully with a spatula so you don't take too much of the air out until it is fully incorporated.

Pour the cake batter onto the prepared baking tray and spread evenly with an offset palette knife. Bake for 5–7 minutes until golden on top. Transfer to a wire rack and leave to cool completely.

While the cake is cooling, make the custard. Whisk the egg yolks, caster sugar, cornflour and vanilla together in a heatproof bowl. Set aside. Bring the milk to simmering point in a small saucepan, then remove from the heat.

cont...

Pour one-quarter of the milk into the egg mixture, whisking constantly to avoid cooking the eggs, then slowly add the rest of the milk. Pour the mixture back into the pan. Return the pan to a low heat and stir for 8–10 minutes until the custard begins to thicken. Remove from the heat, cover the surface of the custard with clingfilm [plastic wrap] and leave to cool completely.

For the mascarpone cream, whip the cream in a stand mixer fitted with the whisk attachment until it just starts to thicken. While whisking, slowly add the icing sugar, then reduce the speed to low and add the mascarpone and vanilla.

Increase the speed to medium-high and beat until the cheese is fully incorporated. Continue whisking until you reach a firm peak consistency. Don't overbeat as the texture will become grainy. Set aside.

Using an 8-cm [3¼-in] round cutter, cut out 6 circles of cake. You will need 3 for each mini tarta.

To build each cake on its own serving plate, spread 1 Tbsp of raspberry jam on the first layer, top with another layer of cake and add the vanilla custard. Add the third cake circle and cover with the mascarpone cream (saving some for decoration) creating a dome and covering the sides of the entire cake. Refrigerate for 30 minutes.

Colour the remaining marzipan in purple or just use purple fondant icing. Roll out the marzipan or fondant to a 3mm [⅛in] thickness and cut out 2 circles each large enough to cover an entire mini cake. Cover each cake, trim the bottom and pipe little flowers or shells of mascarpone cream all around the base.

Pipe a little cream at the top of each cake and place the marzipan legs in the middle. Serve cold.

Jack Frost Vegan Coconut Cake

SERVES 10-12

115g [½ cup] vegan margarine,
plus extra for greasing

200g [1 cup] caster [granulated]
sugar

115g [½ cup] plain vegan yogurt

¼ tsp coconut extract

60ml [¼ cup] coconut milk

1 Tbsp white wine vinegar

225g [1¾ cups] plain
[all-purpose] flour, sifted

1 tsp baking powder

½ tsp bicarbonate of soda
[baking soda]

½ tsp salt

50g [½ cup] sweetened
desiccated [dried shredded]
coconut

Buttercream
100g [½ cup] unsalted vegan
butter, at room temperature

310g [2¼ cups] icing
[confectioners'] sugar, sifted

4 Tbsp coconut milk

¼ tsp coconut extract

1 tsp cocoa powder

black food colour

To decorate
200g [2 cups] desiccated
[dried shredded] coconut,
for sprinkling

clear isomalt

I just can't help but add a little spook to Christmas-themed bakes. They are still recognisably what they are meant to be, in this case a snowman's head but with a mischievous twist. The beauty of a bake like this, is that you can easily make it your own. You don't have to make it look scary, but I know you want to. The vegan sponge is my pride and joy as I spent days getting it right. You would never know this cake is vegan, it has a delicate taste and texture and that's why I recommend refrigerating it before you assemble the cake as the sponge is quite soft.

Preheat the oven to 160°C fan [350°F/Gas mark 4] and grease 2 x 15-cm [6-in] hemisphere cake tins.

Mix the margarine and caster sugar together in a stand mixer on medium speed until light and fluffy. Add the yogurt, coconut extract, coconut milk and vinegar and continue mixing.

Sift the flour, baking powder, bicarbonate of soda and salt together, then slowly add to the wet ingredients on low speed. Add the desiccated coconut and mix until it is fully incorporated. Pour the batter into the prepared cake tins and bake for 35–40 minutes. Leave to cool in the tins for 10 minutes before turning out onto a wire rack.

While the cakes are baking, make the buttercream. Mix the butter and icing sugar together in an electric mixer on medium speed until combined, then slowly add the coconut milk and coconut extract. Turn the speed to high and continue mixing for 4–5 minutes until the buttercream is light and fluffy. If the mixture is too runny, add more icing sugar, and if it's too stiff, add more coconut milk.

cont...

Transfer about 60g [¼ cup] of the buttercream to a small bowl. Mix in the cocoa powder and enough black food colour to get a strong black icing. This will be used for the inside of the eyes and mouth.

Once the cakes are baked and cooled, stick both halves of the sphere together with a layer of buttercream. Apply a crumb coat by coating the cake with a thin layer of icing and smoothing with a bench scraper. Refrigerate for 2–4 hours until set, or ideally overnight.

Apply a second layer of buttercream, accentuating the eyes and cheeks with extra buttercream, and sprinkle all over with desiccated coconut.

Carve out the eyes and mouth and spread the black coloured buttercream on the inside.

Melt the isomalt in the microwave according to the pack instructions. Spread thinly on a silicone mat and let it harden.

Using a large knife, cut the hard isomalt into zigzags to create pointy teeth. They will all be different, but this adds to the creepiness of the character. Attach the teeth to the top and bottom of the mouth.

Sandworm Lemon and Thyme Cupcakes

MAKES 12 CUPCAKES

Sponge

170g [¾ cup] unsalted butter, softened

170g [¾ cup] caster [granulated] sugar

2 large eggs

170g [1¼ cups] self-raising [self-rising] flour, sifted

finely grated zest of 2 unwaxed lemons and juice of 1

2 tsp fresh thyme leaves

Drizzle

120ml [½ cup] water

100g [½ cup] caster [granulated] sugar

juice of 1 lemon

2–3 fresh thyme sprigs

Buttercream

150g [⅔ cup] unsalted butter, at room temperature

finely grated zest and juice of 1 unwaxed lemon

360g [3 cups] icing [confectioners'] sugar, sifted

2 Tbsp sour cream

pink food colour

To decorate

250g [8¾oz] white modelling chocolate, fondant or sugarpaste

black food paint

Those terrible sandworms may haunt your deceased self, but they look rather cute coming out of pink frosting, don't you think? The flavour of these cupcakes is divine – lemon and thyme are not just a savoury combination: it works just as well in cakes. A thyme-infused sugar syrup makes the sponge extra moist. Either use silicone cupcake or muffin cases, or double the paper cases, or carefully transfer the baked cupcakes to new paper cases after adding the drizzle as the syrup will make them sticky.

Preheat the oven to 160°C fan [350°F/Gas mark 4] and line a 12-hole cupcake tray with silicone or paper cases.

Cream the butter and caster sugar together in an electric mixer until light and fluffy. Add the eggs, one by one, and continue mixing until fully incorporated. Reduce the speed to low and add the flour, lemon zest and juice, then add the thyme leaves and continue mixing until all the ingredients come together.

Spoon the batter equally among the cases and bake for 15 minutes, or until a skewer stuck into the middle comes out clean.

Meanwhile, make the drizzle. Put the water and caster sugar into a medium pan over a low-medium heat and once the sugar has dissolved, add the lemon juice and thyme sprigs. Leave it to infuse for a few minutes, then turn off the heat.

Once the cupcakes are ready, take them out of the oven and leave them to cool slightly.

cont...

Poke a few holes in each one with a skewer, then brush the drizzle over them. The paper cases will get wet so make sure to put the cupcakes in new ones after you add the drizzle.

To make the buttercream, cream the butter in an electric mixer until light and fluffy, then add the lemon zest and juice. Continue mixing while slowly adding the sifted icing sugar, then the sour cream. If the buttercream is too thick, add more sour cream and if it's too thin, add more icing sugar. Add enough food colour to achieve a strong pink colour.

Put the buttercream in a piping [pastry] bag with a star nozzle and pipe onto each cupcake.

Mould 36 sandworm 'tentacles' out of modelling chocolate and paint on the stripes with black food paint. Insert 3 tentacles into the buttercream of each cupcake.

Red Riding Wolf Pumpkin Spice Cupcakes

MAKES 18 CUPCAKES

120ml [½ cup] vegetable oil

3 large eggs

230g [1 cup] pumpkin purée

150ml [¾ cup] evaporated milk

2 tsp vanilla extract

240g [2 cups] plain [all-purpose] flour

300g [1½ cups] light brown sugar

2 tsp ground cinnamon

1 tsp ground nutmeg

1 tsp ground ginger

1½ tsp baking powder

1 tsp salt

Buttercream

125g [½ cup] cream cheese, at room temperature

50g [3½ Tbsp] unsalted butter, at room temperature

300g [2½ cups] icing [confectioners'] sugar, sifted

1½ Tbsp maple syrup

½ tsp vanilla extract

To decorate

400g [14oz] red fondant

250g [8¾oz] dark brown modelling chocolate

small amount of Royal Icing (page 81)

1 Tbsp each white and black fondant

purple or blue powder food colour (optional)

These cupcakes represent an alternative ending to the story. The wolf eats the granny AND Red Riding Hood, simply because he desperately wants that gorgeous cape. I don't blame him really, there's not much I wouldn't do for a hooded cape. Pumpkin cupcakes are one of my favourites, and the maple buttercream is the icing on the cake, literally!

Preheat the oven to 170°C fan [375°F/Gas mark 5] and line 2 x 12-hole muffin tins with 18 paper cases.

Mix all the wet ingredients together in an electric mixer on medium speed.

Sift the flour into a large bowl and stir in the other dry ingredients. Slowly add them to the wet ingredients with the mixer on low speed. Keep mixing, scraping down the sides and base of the bowl, until fully incorporated.

Divide the batter equally among the paper cases, filling them three-quarters full. Bake in the centre of the oven for 15 minutes, or until a skewer stuck into them comes out clean. Transfer to a wire rack and leave to cool completely.

To make the buttercream, mix the cream cheese and butter together in an electric mixer on medium-slow speed until light and fluffy. Slowly add the icing sugar and continue mixing. Add the maple syrup and vanilla, then increase the speed to high and mix for a good 3 minutes – be careful not to overmix as it can make the buttercream runny.

Spread a layer of buttercream onto each cupcake using a palette knife and refrigerate while you make the decorations.

cont...

On a surface dusted with icing sugar, roll out the red fondant to a 3mm [⅛in] thickness, then cut 18 circles slightly bigger than the cupcake tops. Cut out an inner circle to give you the red hood. Mould a little red bow too with your fingers and attach.

Cover each cupcake with the red fondant hood.

For the wolf, roll a piece of modelling chocolate into a ball, then mould it slightly into a cone shape. The base will need to be the same circumference as the hole in the red hood.

The cone bit will be the snout of the wolf so bring it down a bit. Once you are happy with the general shape, cut the snout in the middle with scissors to create an open mouth. Stick the wolf heads on top of all the hoods.

Mould 2 little ears out of some more modelling chocolate and attach to the heads.

Use a little red fondant to make the tongue and insert inside the mouth. Pipe the teeth with white royal icing.

Shape the eyes with a little white fondant and add black fondant pupils in the middle. Use more black fondant icing to create the nose.

Pipe the granny's hair with more royal icing and dust in purple to give it a 'blue rinse', if you like. Finally, carve some lines with a toothpick to imitate hair.

Haunted Yule Log

SERVES 8

210g [1¾ cups] plain
[all-purpose] flour

420g [2 cups] caster
[granulated] sugar

90g [¾ cup] cocoa powder

2 tsp bicarbonate of soda
[baking soda]

1 tsp baking powder

1 tsp salt

2 Tbsp smooth peanut butter

120ml [½ cup] vegetable oil

2 large eggs

250ml [1 cup] buttermilk

1 tsp vanilla extract

1½ tsp instant coffee granules

250ml [1 cup] very hot water

Frosting
250g [1 cup] smooth peanut
butter

225g [8oz] cream cheese

1 tsp vanilla extract

¼ tsp salt

375g [3 cups] icing
[confectioners'] sugar

about 2 Tbsp milk

To decorate
1kg [2lb 4oz] dark modelling
chocolate or dark brown
fondant icing

brown food colour

black powder food colour

Turn this Scandinavian classic holiday bake into
a dark fairy tale. Although a yule log is based on a
rolled chocolate sponge, I'm stacking this one. And
since I'm breaking the rules, I'm also adding peanut
butter to the sponge and the frosting. Of course, feel
free to use your favourite chocolate cake recipe for
this idea – I'm just a rebel at heart and I think this
cake is pretty damn tasty.

The day before you want to serve the cake, preheat the
oven to 160°C fan [350°F/Gas mark 4] and oil 4 x 10-cm
[4-in] round cake tins.

Sift the flour, sugar, cocoa, bicarbonate of soda, baking
powder and salt together in a large bowl and set aside.

Cream the peanut butter and oil together in an electric
mixer on medium speed. Add the eggs, one by one,
beating well between each addition. Add the buttermilk
and vanilla and continue mixing.

Turn the mixer to low and add all the dry ingredients.

Dissolve the coffee granules in the hot water and add
to the mixture.

Divide the batter between the prepared tins and bake
for 30–35 minutes until a skewer stuck into the middle
comes out clean. Leave to cool in the tins for 5 minutes
before transferring to a wire rack. Let the cakes cool
completely before frosting.

For the frosting, combine the peanut butter, cream
cheese, vanilla and salt together in an electric mixer.
Add the icing sugar, alternating with the milk until you
get a spreadable consistency. You may not need to use
all the milk.

cont...

Stack the cakes with a layer of the frosting between each cake. Now crumb coat the stack by coating the cake with a layer of frosting and smoothing the side and top with a bench scraper. Secure with a couple of long wooden dowels pushed down through the layers and refrigerate overnight to let it set.

To decorate, roll the modelling chocolate and shape into ropes of different sizes and lengths. This step is quite tedious but it's worth it!

Score the rope pieces with the back of a knife, or use modelling tools if you have them, to imitate tree bark. Stick the pieces onto the cake using frosting. On the front half of the cake, make a dent in the eye and mouth areas (see photo), or create your own expression, such as a Jack O'Lantern or a scared ghost.

Create the arms and base of the tree using more modelling chocolate and blending it into the tree. Mould some around the eyes and cheeks for definition.

Finish the look by painting some brown food colour in the cracks and brushing black powder colour around the inside of the eyes and mouth to create depth.

Tip: If you want to add some turkey tail mushrooms to the side of the cake, mould them out of fondant and paint them with brown edible paint – browse the internet for reference images.

Victoria Sandwitches

MAKES 8 'SANDWITCHES'

Sponge
100ml [½ cup] vegetable oil

300g [1½ cups] caster [granulated] sugar

2 large eggs

1 tsp vanilla extract

320g [2¼ cups] plain [all-purpose] flour, sifted

2½ tsp baking powder

1 tsp salt

240ml [1 cup] whole milk

Filling
raspberry jam

about 200ml [¾ cup] double [heavy] cream, whipped

Witches' hats
6 Oreo cookies

200g [7oz] dark chocolate, chopped into small pieces

black sanding sugar (available online), for sprinkling and rolling

12 original-flavour Bugles [cone-shaped corn snacks]

Unless you eat a Victoria sandwich cake straight away, you will find that it becomes dry rather quickly, so I've come up with an alternative for the sponge. It looks very similar, but I think it tastes much better and stays fresher for longer. I've shaped the cakes into actual 'sandwitches', each topped with a little witch's hat. It is not complicated at all to do and will look incredible at a witches' tea party.

Preheat the oven to 180°C fan [400°F/Gas mark 6] and line a 25 x 25-cm [10 x 10-in] baking tin with baking paper.

To make the sponge, mix the oil and sugar together in an electric mixer until light and fluffy. Add the eggs, one by one, mixing well between each addition, then add the vanilla extract.

Sift the flour, baking powder and salt into a bowl, then add one-third to the sugar mixture. Mix, then add one-third of the milk and mix again. Repeat, alternating flour and milk, until all used up. Transfer the batter to the prepared tin and bake for 20–25 minutes until a skewer stuck into the middle comes out clean.

Leave the cake to cool slightly in the tin, then remove and leave to cool completely on a wire rack.

When the cake is completely cooled, level the top and edges of the sponge, then divide it into 4 squares – use a ruler – with a sharp knife.

Slice each square horizontally to create 2 slices of 'sandwich' bread, then fill with jam and whipped cream. Press both slices together and cut diagonally to create a triangle sandwich. Repeat with the other squares.

To make the witches hats, separate the cookies and remove the filling.

Melt the chocolate in a microwaveable bowl in the microwave at 30-second intervals. Dip each cookie half into the chocolate, then sprinkle with sanding sugar and place on baking paper.

Dip the Bugles into the melted chocolate, then roll in the sugar and attach to the cookie base using more melted chocolate, if necessary.

Attach each hat to the side of the sandwiches with a little melted chocolate to convert them into 'sandwitches'.

Vanilla Coffin Cakes

MAKES 2 MEDIUM CAKES OR
4 SMALL ONES / SERVES 4

95g [½ cup] unsalted butter,
softened

95ml [½ cup] vegetable oil

135g [¾ cup] caster [granulated]
sugar

120ml [½ cup] sour cream

60ml [¼ cup] whole milk

1 Tbsp vanilla extract

2 large eggs

220g [1⅔ cups] plain
[all-purpose] flour, sifted

1½ tsp baking powder

½ tsp bicarbonate of soda
[baking soda]

½ tsp salt

Royal Icing (page 81–2),
to decorate (optional)

Buttercream
240g [1 cup] unsalted butter,
softened

480g [3⅓ cups] icing
[confectioners'] sugar, sifted

2 Tbsp sour cream

1 Tbsp vanilla extract

1 tsp salt

pink, purple and yellow food
colours, or your choice

These individual cakes are decorated with swirls
of pastel buttercream and remind me of the 1970s'
revival of Edwardian fashion – frilly, lacy and
fancy. What's not to love? The sponge is my go-to
vanilla cake recipe, which is wonderfully moist and
uncomplicated, but so delicious.

Preheat the oven to 170°C fan [375°F/Gas mark 5] and
line a 27 x 18-cm [10¾ x 7-in] rectangular baking tin
with baking paper.

Beat the butter, oil and sugar in a stand mixer, or use a
handheld electric whisk, until light and fluffy. Add the
sour cream, milk and vanilla and beat until combined,
then add the eggs, one by one, mixing well between
each addition.

Add the flour, baking powder, bicarbonate of soda
and salt and mix, scraping down the sides and base of
the bowl occasionally, until completely combined. Do
not overmix.

Pour the batter into the prepared tin and bake for
20–25 minutes until a toothpick comes out clean.

Leave the cake to cool slightly in the tin, then tip it
out onto a wire rack and leave until completely cooled.
Level the cake with a serrated knife.

Draw a coffin shape, about 19 x 9cm [7½ x 3½in] (for
the larger ones) or 13 x 7cm [5 x 2¾in] (for the smaller
version) on a piece of paper and use it as a template to
cut out your cakes.

To make the buttercream, beat the butter in an electric
mixer until light and fluffy. Add the icing sugar, sour
cream, vanilla and salt and continue mixing until
everything is incorporated.

Divide the buttercream among 4 different bowls and add food colour to 3 bowls. Make sure you add the colour a little at a time as we are going for pastel shades here. Reserve the white buttercream to use for decorative scrolls and lines, or use royal icing instead.

Apply pastel buttercream to the sides and top of each coffin cake and decorate with white buttercream or royal icing. The designs are up to you; I did a cross for one and a grid pattern for the other two featured in the photo.

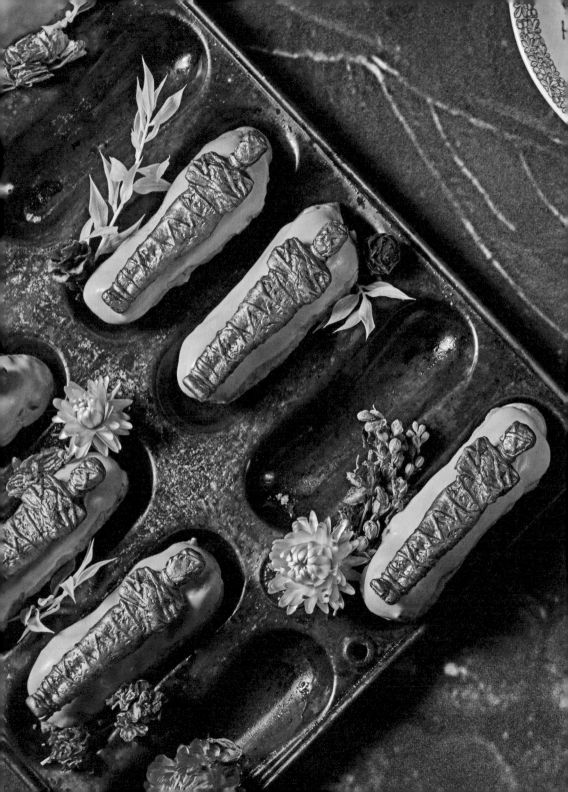

Pies & Pastries

Yummy Mummy Éclairs

MAKES 16 ÉCLAIRS

Choux pastry

185g [1½ cups] plain [all-purpose] flour, sifted

1 Tbsp caster [granulated] sugar

250ml [1 cup] water

125g [½ cup] salted butter

4 extra-large eggs, beaten

Filling

150g [1 cup] blueberries

75g [⅓ cup] caster [granulated] sugar

250ml [1 cup] whipping cream

finely grated zest of ½ unwaxed lemon

2 Tbsp lemon juice

To decorate

200g [7oz] white modelling chocolate

gold edible paint

200g [7oz] white chocolate, chopped

green or blue cocoa base food colour

edible flowers

For this project you will need a silicone mummy mould. I found mine online. I have chosen a blueberry lemon filling for these, but if you prefer use crème pâtissière or any other filling instead.

Preheat the oven to 200°C fan [425°F/Gas mark 7].

First, make the mummies using the modelling chocolate and mould. Paint gold and let dry completely – 2 hours.

Make the choux pastry exactly the same way as on page 44, but this time, pipe it into 16 straight lines on a silicone mat or in an éclair baking tin. Reduce the oven to 180°C fan [400°F/Gas mark 6] and bake for 25–30 minutes until golden brown. Remove from the oven and prick a hole in the base of each éclair to release the steam. Reduce the oven to 160°C fan [350°F/Gas mark 4] and bake the éclairs for 5–8 minutes to dry out. Let cool completely.

For the filling, cook the blueberries and sugar in a pan over a low-medium heat until the berries start breaking down. Blend in a food processor until smooth, then pass the puree through a sieve. Set aside.

Whip the cream to soft peak stage, then add the lemon zest and juice. Stir in the blueberry puree and spoon into a piping [pastry] bag. Make 3 holes in the base of each éclair and pipe in the filling.

Melt the white chocolate either in the microwave at 30-second intervals or in a heatproof bowl set over a pan of simmering water, making sure the base of the bowl isn't touching the water, then colour it green or blue. Dip the top of each éclair into the chocolate, then leave to set slightly on a wire rack, attaching the mummy before the chocolate sets completely.

Decorate the mummies with flowers.

* Photographed on previous spread

Death of a Royal Swan Pie

SERVES 2-3

750g [5 cups] fresh raspberries

170g [¾ cup] caster [granulated] sugar

2 Tbsp cornflour [cornstarch]

juice of ½ lemon

flour, for dusting

2 x 320-g [11½-oz] packets of ready-rolled vegan (non-butter) shortcrust pastry

water or non-dairy milk, for attaching

vegan vanilla ice cream, to serve

To decorate

2 wooden skewers, soaked in water for 30 minutes

50g [1¾oz] good-quality dark chocolate, melted

black edible paint or edible ink pen

This is an ideal pie to serve as dessert for a Valentine's dinner for two. Until very recently, killing a swan in Britain was considered treason and, still now, wild swans are protected by the crown.

I wanted to represent the killing of a swan in pie form, inspired by Victorian meat pies when they used to attach the actual wings of the bird to the pastry! No need for that here, we are making them out of shortcrust. And ironically, this pie is vegan.

Preheat the oven to 170°C fan [375°F/Gas mark 5].

Cook the raspberries, sugar, cornflour and lemon juice together in a saucepan over a medium heat until the raspberries start to break down and the mixture thickens (if it's too runny it will leak out of the pie) – about 5–8 minutes. Remove from the heat and leave to cool.

Dust your work surface with some flour and roll out the first pack of pastry to a 3mm [⅛in] thickness. Cut out pieces to fit the base and sides of a large pork pie-style tin, about 8cm [3¼in] tall and 10cm [4in] in diameter. Use the offcuts to cut out a disc for the lid. Use the pieces to line the tin and fill with the raspberry mixture. Top with the lid and seal the edges with your thumb. Make a little hole in the centre to let the steam out and bake for 30–40 minutes until golden brown.

Use the rest of the pastry offcuts to mould a swan's head and neck. I simply looked online for a picture of a swan and used it as reference. Make sure the total length is just slightly longer than the height of your tin. Cover with clingfilm [plastic wrap] and refrigerate for 30 minutes before baking.

Roll out the second pack of pastry to a 3mm [⅛in] thickness. We will make the wings and arrows with this

cont...

one. To make the wings, draw the shape of a wing on a piece of paper, then use this as an outline to cut 2 wings out of the pastry. Using a sharp knife, score feathers onto the pastry wings.

Cut out little circles of pastry, give them a few feathery lines and attach them to the base of the wing with a little water or non-dairy milk. Make some single feathers, some large and some small, for the front base of the pie.

For the arrows, cut the arrow heads out of pastry and insert a wooden skewer through the middle. Place the wings on a baking tray lined with baking paper, and the feathers and arrows on a separate lined baking tray and refrigerate everything for 15 minutes.

Put the swan head on a separate lined baking tray, then transfer to the oven with the wings, feathers and arrows. They will bake at different speeds – the wings, feathers and arrows will only take about 20 minutes until they turn golden brown, so keep an eye on them. Leave the head for a bit longer, checking every few minutes.

Once all the elements are baked, use the melted chocolate to attach the wings to the sides of the pie. Attach the large feathers to the sides of the front, and the smaller ones on top and above. Leave space for the head.

Finally, paint the eyes with a small brush or use an edible ink pen and attach the head to the front of the pie with a little more chocolate. Serve with vanilla ice cream.

Pumpkin and Orange Empanadas

MAKES 12 EMPANADAS

500g [4 cups] plain [all-purpose] flour, plus extra for dusting

1 tsp salt

½ Tbsp caster [granulated] sugar

45g [3 Tbsp] salted butter, melted

220ml [1 cup minus 1 Tbsp] lukewarm water

vegetable oil, for deep-frying

Filling
230g [8oz] pumpkin or butternut squash

3 Tbsp sugar

60ml [¼ cup] water

100g [1 cup] ground almonds

115g [½ cup] caster [granulated] sugar

finely grated zest of 2 oranges

If Spain had its own version of Harry Potter, these would be their pumpkin pasties. This recipe can easily be made vegan by substituting the pastry with shop-bought shortcrust or using vegan margarine. If pumpkin is out of season, just use butternut squash. The filling is Michael's (from my *Bake Off* year) invention – he used it to fill little filo [phyllo] pastry parcels, which is a healthier alternative.

Place the flour in a large bowl, add the salt and sugar and mix with your fingertips. Add the melted butter and lukewarm water and mix with your hands. Continue kneading the dough in the bowl for about 5 minutes until it forms a ball. Cover the bowl with clingfilm [plastic wrap] or a clean towel and leave to rest at room temperature for 30 minutes.

Meanwhile, make the filling. Peel and cut the pumpkin into 1-cm [½-in] chunks. Add to a small saucepan with the 3 Tbsp sugar and water and heat over a medium heat. Cook until the pumpkin is soft and the liquid has evaporated.

Pulse the ground almonds, caster sugar and orange zest several times in a food processor. Add the cooked pumpkin and continue pulsing until a paste forms.

Roll the dough out on a floured surface until it is 3mm [⅛in] thick. Cut out 24 pumpkin shapes using a cookie cutter or a paper template. Fill half the shapes with 1–2 tsp of the filling and spread it to 5mm [¼in] from the edge, then place another pumpkin over the top and seal the edges tightly with a fork.

Heat the oil for deep-frying in a deep-fryer or a large, deep saucepan to 180°C [350°F], or until a cube of bread dropped in sizzles in 30 seconds. Deep-fry the empanadas in small batches until golden brown, then remove and drain on paper towels. Serve warm.

Flying Bats Croquembouche

Choux pastry

185g [1½ cups] plain [all-purpose] flour, sifted

1 Tbsp caster [granulated] sugar

½ tsp salt

450ml [1¾ cups] water

175g [¾ cup] unsalted butter

6 large eggs, beaten

Filling

250g [2 cups] fresh raspberries

150g [¾ cup] caster [granulated] sugar

500ml [2 cups] whipping cream

To decorate

6–8 rice/wafer paper sheets

air brush with black food colour; or activated charcoal mixed with vegetable oil; or black powder food colour

white edible ink pen

400g [2 cups] caster [granulated] sugar

100ml [½ cup] water

27-cm [10¾-in] tall polystyrene cone

I have been wanting to do this for ages and finally I have an excuse. Each little choux bun has bat wings made out of rice paper and is filled with raspberry cream. I recommend you make the wings on one day and the baking on another as it's a time-consuming task. This is a centrepiece dessert that will sure get the coven talking.

Preheat the oven to 200°C fan [425°F/Gas mark 7] and line 2 baking trays with baking paper.

For the choux pastry, combine the flour, sugar and salt together in a small bowl.

Pour the water into a saucepan over a low-medium heat, add the butter and stir until melted. Bring to a quick boil, then stir in the flour mixture all at once with a wooden spoon. Stir vigorously until the dough comes off the sides of the pan and forms a ball.

Transfer the dough to an electric mixer and mix on slow speed until the dough cools down, about 3–4 minutes. Start adding the beaten eggs slowly until you get a glossy dough that holds its shape. You may not need to use all the egg.

Spoon the mixture into a large piping [pastry] bag with a plain round tip and pipe balls of pastry onto the prepared baking trays. Wet your finger and smooth out any peaks.

Reduce the oven to 180°C fan [400°F/Gas mark 6] and bake for 25–30 minutes until golden brown. Remove from the oven and prick a hole in the base of each choux bun with a skewer to release the steam.

Reduce the oven to 160°C fan [350°F/Gas mark 4] and bake the choux buns for another 5–8 minutes to dry out. Remove from the oven and leave to cool completely.

cont...

Meanwhile, to make the filling, heat the raspberries and half the sugar together in a saucepan over a medium heat until they start to break down and the mixture thickens – about 5 minutes. Transfer the mixture to a food processor and blend until smooth, then pass it through a sieve to remove the pips. Set aside.

Pour the whipping cream into an electric mixer and beat to soft peak stage while slowly adding the remaining sugar. Using a spatula, mix in the raspberry pulp, then spoon into a piping bag.

Use the tip of the piping bag to slightly enlarge the hole in the base of each choux bun. Pipe the raspberry filling into the buns.

To create the bat wings you will need first to colour the rice/wafer paper black. If you don't have an airbrush, mix some activated charcoal with a little vegetable oil and use a brush to paint it on. It will give the paper a watercolour effect, which I rather like. Alternatively, you can brush black edible powder over it. Make sure to paint front and back. Fold each paper sheet vertically and, using a paper template or a cookie cutter, draw bat wings up against the fold of the paper with the white edible ink pen. Cut as many as you need depending on how many choux buns you have baked.

To make a caramel, put the sugar and water into a medium saucepan on low-medium heat and stir until the sugar dissolves. Turn the heat up to medium and boil, making sure you clean the sides of the pan with a wet pastry brush to avoid crystallization. Once the sugar turns amber, take off the heat.

Use a little of the caramel to – carefully! the caramel will be very hot – attach the cone to your desired serving plate, then glue each pair of wings to a choux bun with a little more caramel. Attach the choux buns to the cone, starting at the base and building it up in circles. Drizzle the remaining caramel over the croquembouche.

Spiderweb-Top Mince Pies

MAKES 12

230g [1¾ cups] plain [all-purpose] flour, plus extra for dusting

135g [⅔ cup] cold salted butter, cubed

2 Tbsp caster [granulated] sugar

2 large egg yolks

1 Tbsp cold water (optional)

non-stick spray, for greasing

1 whole egg, for brushing

1 egg, lightly beaten, for glazing

Demerara sugar, for sprinkling

Filling

400g [14oz] jar of good-quality mincemeat

finely grated zest of 1 small unwaxed lemon

1 small apple, cored and finely chopped

handful of pecan nuts, roughly chopped

This is an easy and effective way to give a little spooky touch to a Christmas classic. In Germany spiders play a big role at Christmas due to the story of the little spider who decorated the Christmas tree with its web. (Apparently this is where the tradition of decorating the tree with tinsel comes from.)

Sift the flour into a medium bowl, add the cubed butter and rub it into the flour with your fingertips until it resembles breadcrumbs. Alternatively, pulse in a food processor.

Add the caster sugar and egg yolks and mix with your hands until the dough is just coming together, adding the cold water if necessary. Do not overmix.

Flatten the pastry into a disc and wrap in clingfilm [plastic wrap]. Chill in the fridge for 15 minutes while you prepare the filling.

Preheat the oven to 180°C fan [400°F/Gas mark 6]. Grease a 12-hole muffin tin with non-stick spray.

To make the filling, pour the mincemeat into a large bowl, add the lemon zest, apple and pecans and mix until fully incorporated.

Roll out the pastry on a lightly floured surface until it is 3mm [⅛in] thick. Cut out 12 pastry discs with a circumference slightly bigger your tin holes, then press each disc into the holes. Fill each one with the mincemeat mixture.

cont...

Cut out another 12 discs, a little smaller this time, for the tops. Stamp out with a spiderweb cutter if you have one, or simply draw on a spiderweb design with a pastry tool or sharp knife.

Brush the rims of each pastry case with beaten egg and press the lids on top. Seal around the edges with a fork or your little finger. Poke a hole in the middle to allow the steam to escape, then brush the tops with the remaining beaten egg and sprinkle with Demerara sugar.

Bake for 20–25 minutes until golden brown. Leave to cool in the tin for 10 minutes, then transfer to a wire rack and leave to cool completely.

Moon Witch Blackberry Pie

SERVES 6-8

300g [2½ cups] plain [all-purpose] flour, plus extra for dusting

½ tsp salt

1 tsp icing [confectioners'] sugar

225g [1 cup] unsalted butter, cut into cubes

4–5 Tbsp ice-cold water

1 egg yolk, for brushing

Filling
800g [5–6 cups] fresh blackberries

100g [½ cup] caster [granulated] sugar, plus extra if needed

1 Tbsp cornflour [cornstarch]

1 tsp lemon juice

1 tsp ground cinnamon

1 Tbsp ground almonds

This pie can easily be made vegan by using shop-bought non-butter shortcrust pastry instead, and brushing the pastry with vegan milk. If in season, I highly recommend picking your own blackberries. There's something rather special about foraging your ingredients from the wild and magically transforming them into a sweet treat.

Pulse the flour, salt and icing sugar together in a food processor a couple of times to mix together. Add the cubed butter and pulse until the mixture resembles breadcrumbs (alternatively, do this with your hands). Add the water, 1 Tbsp at a time, until the mixture forms large clumps and holds together when you press it.

Dust your work surface with flour and tip the dough out onto it. Knead it a couple of times to bring it together. Form into a ball, flatten it, cover in clingfilm [plastic wrap] and refrigerate while you make the filling.

For the filling, combine the blackberries, sugar, cornflour, lemon juice and cinnamon and leave for 15 minutes.

Preheat the oven to 170°C fan [375°F/Gas mark 5]. You will need a 23-cm [9-in] pie dish.

Divide the pastry into 2 portions, one slightly bigger for the base of the dish. Roll out the larger piece on a lightly floured surface to a 3mm [⅛in] thickness and use it to line the pie dish. Cover with clingfilm and refrigerate while you make the top. Roll out the remaining pastry and cut out a flying witch silhouette, a crescent moon and some little stars using a paper template. You can cut out other shapes, if you like.

Sprinkle the ground almonds over the base of the pie and top with the blackberry mixture. Top with the cut-out shapes and brush them with the egg yolk. Bake for 30–35 minutes until golden brown. If the top is cooking quicker than the bottom, cover with foil. Serve hot.

Eye of Horus Chocolate Tarts

MAKES 8-10 MINI TARTS

Chocolate custard

6 Tbsp golden [light corn] syrup

250g [8¾oz] milk chocolate (it has to be Cadbury's), chopped

200g [¾ cup plus 2 Tbsp] butter, cubed

4 large eggs

To decorate
flour, for dusting

375-g [13-oz] packet ready-rolled shortcrust pastry

8-10 black seedless grapes

1 egg, lightly beaten, for glazing

black edible paint

The most delicious treacle chocolate filling makes these tarts so rich and decadent. The original recipe belonged to my best friend's mum who bakes it without any pastry and simply tops it with flaked [slivered] almonds. Since you only need a little pastry for the decoration, I wouldn't bother making it unless you already have some in the freezer.

Preheat the oven to 140°C fan [325°F/Gas mark 3].

Heat the golden syrup in a medium non-stick pan over a low-medium heat. Add the chocolate and let it melt, stirring occasionally. Remove the pan from the heat and add the butter. Leave it to melt, then add the eggs, one by one, and mix until combined.

Divide the mixture between 8–10 foil pie cases or ramekins and bake for 30 minutes.

Meanwhile, dust your work surface with flour and roll out the pastry until it is 3mm [⅛in] thick. Cut out 8–10 circles the same diameter as the top of the pie cases or ramekins. Place a grape in the middle of the pastry circle, then cut out the eye lids from the leftover pastry and stick around the grapes with a little beaten egg. Add the remaining decorative touches to finish the eye, as per the photo, then brush with more beaten egg and carefully place the lids on top of the cases. Return to the oven for a further 15 minutes, or until golden brown.

Once the pies are cool, paint the eye decorations with black paint.

Vegan Cream Horn Shells with Vampire Crabs

MAKES 8 CREAM HORNS

Pastry horns
vegetable oil, for oiling

375-g [13-oz] packet ready-rolled vegan (not all-butter) puff pastry

Coconut cream filling
400-g [14-oz] can good-quality coconut cream or milk

60g [½ cup] icing [confectioners'] sugar, sifted

To decorate
250g [8¾oz] white modelling chocolate

orange powder food colour

black and white writing icing

icing [confectioners'] sugar, for dusting

I made these last summer and they were a total hit! I've always seen cream horns as seashells anyway, so I wanted to bring that vision to life with these. Don't be put off by the moulding of the crabs – it's very easy; I have absolutely no experience in sculpting, so just looked at a picture for reference. Even if they come out looking odd, it adds character to the bake. I tend to make the crabs the day before, so they harden, but the coconut cream also needs to be refrigerated overnight.

The day before you bake the horns, make the crabs. Using the modelling chocolate, mould the shape of the crab, starting with a cone-like body and adding the arms and pincers. Colour with orange powder, then pipe the eyes with the black writing icing and the fangs with the white. Leave to harden at room temperature overnight.

At the same time, put the coconut cream or milk in the fridge to chill overnight. This is an essential step in order to separate the fats from the milk.

The next day, preheat the oven to 180°C fan [400°F/Gas mark 6] and line a baking tray with baking paper. Oil 8 cream horn moulds.

Unroll the puff pastry and cut it lengthways into 1-cm [½-in] wide strips. Starting at the tip, wrap the pastry strips around the moulds, overlapping them slightly. Place the horns on their sides on the prepared baking tray and bake for 10–12 minutes until golden brown.

Leave to cool completely on a wire rack before removing from the moulds. Set aside.

cont...

Remove the coconut cream from the fridge, scrape out the solids at the top and place in an electric mixer. Mix for about 1 minute while slowly adding the icing sugar; the mixture will become creamy. Taste for sweetness and adapt to your liking.

Put the filling into a piping [pastry] bag fitted with a star nozzle and pipe into the cones. Place on top of the crabs, then dust with icing sugar to finish.

Tip: you can buy cream horn moulds in specialist kitchen stores and online.

Cousin Itt Baklava

MAKES 4

200g [1½ cups] shelled
pistachios, chopped

1 tsp ground cinnamon

pinch of ground cloves

450g [1lb] kataifi dough, thawed

4 Tbsp butter or vegan spread,
melted

Syrup

300ml [1¼ cups] water

450g [2¼ cups] granulated
sugar

peel of ½ clementine

1 cinnamon stick

To decorate

small amount of shortbread or
gingerbread dough (see page 81)

boiled sweets [candies], crushed

black fondant icing

I once found shredded filo [phyllo] pastry in the frozen section of an Asian grocery store, so I bought it thinking I would use it at some point. The eureka moment came a few weeks later. The pastry is called 'kataifi' and it's used in Greek and Turkish cuisines. It is available online too, and you can get very creative with it. Cousin Itt's hat is made from black fondant icing and his glasses are made from gingerbread dough for the frames and boiled sweets [candies] for the glass.

Preheat the oven to 170°C fan [375°F/Gas mark 5] and line a baking tray with baking paper.

Pulse the pistachios, cinnamon and cloves in a food processor a few times to combine all the ingredients and chop the nuts. Do not over-process.

Make sure the pastry is completely thawed out before you start. Unroll it and, using a sharp knife, divide it into four 25-cm [10-in] portions.

Take one portion and pull the strands apart to make them fluffy, then brush a little melted butter onto one half of the portion. Spoon one-quarter of the pistachio mixture on the bottom portion and fold the other half over. Shape with your hands to get a rough cone-like structure.

Repeat the process with the rest of the pastry, then place all 4 Cousin Itts on the prepared baking tray. Bake for 40 minutes, or until the pastry is crispy.

For the syrup, heat the water, sugar, clementine peel and cinnamon stick together in a saucepan over a medium heat. Once the sugar dissolves, simmer for 3–4 minutes.

cont...

As soon as the pastries are ready, remove them from the oven and ladle the syrup over the top of each one.

Cut out the glasses from the gingerbread dough, using a small (around 2.5cm [1in]) round cutter if you have it, and a slightly smaller one to take out an inner circle. Alternatively, you can cut out the shape of the glasses carefully, by hand, using a small, sharp knife. Make 4 sets of glasses frames.

Place the glasses frames on a lined baking tray, then fill the inner circle with crushed boiled sweets and bake in the oven for 7 minutes or until the sweets melt to form 'glass'.

Mould 4 bowler hats by hand using black fondant icing.

To attach the glasses, melt some more of the crushed boiled sweets in the oven and use them as glue, but do not touch the molten sweets with your bare skin!

Traditional Pumpkin Pie

SERVES 8-10

350g [12oz] shortcrust pastry (or use the pastry recipe on page 51)

handful of whole cloves (optional)

425g [15oz] pumpkin purée

1 large egg, plus 1 egg yolk

235ml [1 cup] evaporated milk

200g [1 cup] caster [granulated] sugar

1 tsp salt

1 tsp ground cinnamon, plus extra to decorate

¼ tsp ground ginger

¼ tsp ground cloves

1 Tbsp plain [all-purpose] flour, plus extra for dusting

1 egg, lightly beaten, for glazing

whipped cream, to serve (optional)

This one is for the Brits. Having lived in America, I know there's little point in adding a pumpkin pie recipe here for Americans, but the British are still to discover the wonders of this dish. Incredibly simple to make and an ode to autumn. If you have never made pumpkin pie before, please, give it a go.

Preheat the oven to 170°C fan [375°F/Gas mark 5].

Dust your work surface with flour and roll out the pastry to a 3mm [⅛in] thickness, then use it to line a 24-cm [9½-in] pie dish or quiche tin and trim the edges with a sharp knife.

Use the pastry off-cuts to make some pumpkins – roll little balls of the pastry, then squash them a little and use the back of a knife to form ridges. Use cloves for the stalks, or alternatively make the stalks out of more pastry. For the leaves, roll out the pastry and use a leaf pastry cutter to stamp out leaves, or cut them out by hand. Roll some pastry into ropes to create vines. Arrange the decorations on a baking tray lined with baking paper.

Using a wooden spoon or spatula, mix the pumpkin purée, egg, egg yolk, evaporated milk, sugar, salt, spices and flour together in a medium bowl. Pour into the pastry case. Brush the edge of the pastry crust and all the decorations with the beaten egg. Put the pie and decorations in the oven. Bake the decorations for 10–15 minutes and the pie itself for 30–40 minutes until the filling is set.

Leave the pie to cool, then decorate with the pastry pumpkins, leaves and vines. Dust with cinnamon and serve with whipped cream, if you like.

Breads & Enriched Doughs

Devilish Donuts

MAKES 12 DONUTS

300g [2½ cups] plain [all-purpose] flour, sifted, plus extra for dusting

40g [¼ cup] caster [granulated] sugar

7-g [14-oz] sachet of fast-action dried [active dry] yeast

¼ tsp salt

160ml [⅔ cup] milk

60g [¼ cup] salted butter

1 egg

1 tsp vanilla extract

Glaze

200g [7oz] white chocolate

150ml [⅔ cup] double [heavy] cream

red cocoa base food colour

To decorate

24 unsalted cashew nuts or blanched almonds

black edible paint

These rather naughty-looking donuts are actually not that bad for you as they are baked rather than fried. And despite their devilish look they are lovely, fluffy and sweet. I couldn't help myself and I carved the horns out of blanched almonds using a sharp knife, but you could just use cashew nuts instead as they have a horn shape anyway. I just wanted very pointy ends.

For the donuts, place the flour, sugar, yeast and salt in a stand mixer fitted with a dough hook attachment.

Warm the milk in a saucepan, then add the butter and heat until the butter is completely melted. Remove from the heat and leave to cool to lukewarm, about 40°C [104°F].

Turn the mixer to medium speed and mix the dry ingredients together, then add the egg, milk and butter mixture and vanilla and mix until the dough comes off the sides of the bowl. Cover the bowl with clingfilm [plastic wrap] or a clean towel and leave to rise in a warm place for 1–1½ hours, or until doubled in size. Line a baking tray with baking paper.

Knock back the risen dough with your hand, turn it onto a lightly floured surface and roll it out to about 1cm [½in] thickness. Cut out 12 circles, re-rolling if necessary, with a round 8.5-cm [3¼-in] cookie cutter. Using a smaller, 4-cm [1½-in] cutter, cut out a hole in the middle of each circle. Place on the prepared baking tray, cover with clingfilm or a towel and leave to rise in a warm place again for 45 minutes.

Preheat the oven to 180°C fan [400°F/Gas mark 6].

Bake the donuts for 10–12 minutes until golden brown. Leave to cool on a wire rack before glazing.

For the glaze, roughly chop 150g [5oz] of the white chocolate and set aside in a large heatproof bowl.

Bring the cream to a simmer in a saucepan over a low-medium heat. Don't let it boil. Pour the cream onto the chocolate and stir until completely melted. Stir in enough red food colour to make the glaze a strong red.

Dip the tops of the donuts, one by one, into the chocolate mixture and leave to stand on a wire rack until the glaze is fully set – about 20 minutes.

Melt the remaining 50g [2oz] chocolate in a heatproof bowl in the microwave at 20-second intervals. (Alternatively, set over a saucepan of gently simmering water, making sure the base of the bowl doesn't touch the water.) Stir in red food colour, then pour into a small piping [pastry] bag with a small tip. Pipe the devil's forked tail onto the set donuts.

For the horns, if using cashew nuts simply paint them black and insert them on top of the ring donuts. If using almonds, carve into horn shape with a sharp knife and then paint and insert.

* Photographed on previous spread

Double Chocolate Spiderweb Buns

MAKES 8 BUNS

oil, for oiling

220ml [1 cup] whole milk, warmed to 35–40°C [95–104°F]

1 tsp fast-action dried [active dry] yeast

110g [½ cup] caster [granulated] sugar

320g [2¼ cups] strong white bread flour, plus extra for dusting

1 tsp Pumpkin Spice Mix (page 115)

25g [¼ cup] cocoa powder

40g [3 Tbsp] butter, melted

1 small egg

75g [½ cup] dark chocolate chips

Piping mixture
60g [⅓ cup plus 1 Tbsp] strong white bread flour

2 tsp caster [superfine] sugar

60ml [¼ cup] water

Glaze
50g [¼ cup] caster [granulated] sugar

1½ Tbsp water

½ tsp vanilla extract

To serve
butter

honey or maple syrup

I created these hot cross buns in an attempt to make Easter spooky. Piping spiderwebs rather than crosses is a simple way to bring a touch of your favourite holiday into another. I love to toast these, butter them and then top them with honey – breakfast for witches!

Oil a large bowl well and set aside. Add all the ingredients, except the chocolate chips, to an electric mixer fitted with the paddle attachment and knead on low-medium speed for about 5 minutes until a dough forms. The dough will be sticky. Transfer to the oiled bowl and cover with clingfilm [plastic wrap] or a clean towel. Leave to rise in a warm place for 1½ hours, or until doubled in size. Meanwhile, grease a 30-cm [12-in] long baking tray or dish, or line with baking paper.

Knock back the dough on a lightly floured surface, then knead in the chocolate chips. Divide the dough into 8 equal pieces and roll them into balls. Place them on the prepared baking tray, leaving a 1-cm [½-in] gap between them, then cover with clingfilm or a towel and leave to prove in a warm place again for 45 minutes, or until doubled in size.

Preheat the oven to 180°C fan [400°F/Gas mark 6].

Prepare the piping mixture by combining all the ingredients. Mix well with a fork, then pour into a piping [pastry] bag with a small nozzle.

After the buns have finished proving, pipe a spiderweb on top of each one, then bake for 10 minutes. Reduce the oven to 170°C fan [375°F/Gas mark 5] and bake for 25–30 minutes. Transfer to a wire rack to cool slightly.

To make the glaze, combine all the ingredients in a small saucepan over a low heat and stir until the sugar has dissolved. Brush the glaze onto the warm buns, then serve toasted with butter and honey or maple syrup.

Tangled Snake Cinnamon Pretzels

MAKES 6 PRETZELS

240ml [1 cup] whole milk, warmed to 35–40°C [95–104°F]

7-g [¼-oz] sachet of fast-action dried [active dry] yeast

1 Tbsp soft brown sugar

1 Tbsp unsalted butter, melted and cooled, plus extra for glazing

300g [2½ cups] plain [all-purpose] flour

1 tsp salt

1 litre [4 cups] water

110g [½ cup] bicarbonate of soda [baking soda]

12 black peppercorns

100g [½ cup] caster [granulated] sugar

2 Tbsp ground cinnamon

red and green food colours

edible rice paper, painted with red food colour

Royal Icing (page 81–2) or edible glue

I've always seen the shape of pretzels as tangled snakes. If you've never made pretzels before, definitely give them a go – they are not as scary as they seem, and even in a snake shape they look rather cute. To make them sweet, sprinkle with green coloured cinnamon sugar and for savoury, colour grated Parmesan instead. I've opted for cinnamon sugar here.

Place the warm milk in an electric mixer fitted with a dough hook attachment, then sprinkle in the yeast. Leave to soften for about 1 minute, then add the brown sugar and butter.

Mix the flour and salt together. Turn the mixer on and add the salted flour, one-third at a time, mixing between additions. Knead for about 3 minutes until the dough comes together, adding more flour if necessary, but you are looking for a tacky dough. Cover the bowl with a clean towel and leave to rise in a warm place for about 1 hour, or until doubled in size.

Preheat the oven to 200°C fan [425°F/Gas mark 7].

Knock back the dough on a lightly floured surface, then divide it into 6 equal pieces.

Roll each piece into a 30–35-cm [12–14-in] rope, stretching and slapping the dough down, then form into a pretzel knot shape with a larger end for the head and a thinner end for the tail of the snake.

Line a baking tray with baking paper. Bring the water with the bicarbonate of soda to the boil in a large pan. Drop 2 pretzels at a time into the boiling water and cook for about 30 seconds, then remove and place on the prepared baking tray.

cont...

Reshape each pretzel, pinching the dough at the thicker end to form the snake head and defining the pointed end for the tail. Add 2 peppercorns for the eyes. Bake the pretzels for 10–12 minutes until golden brown.

Meanwhile, to make the cinnamon sugar, mix the caster sugar and cinnamon together in a small bowl and colour with the green food colour. Rub the colour in with your hands until it is fully incorporated. I recommend wearing latex gloves for this.

Cut some little snake tongues from the red rice paper.

Transfer the pretzels to a wire rack when they come out of the oven. Brush some extra melted butter over them. Sprinkle with the green cinnamon sugar, avoiding the heads, and stick the tongues on with a little royal icing or edible glue.

Bat Scones with Berried Alive Syrup

MAKES 6-8 SCONES

225g [1¾ cups] self-raising [self-rising] flour, plus extra for dusting

½ tsp baking powder

¼ tsp salt

75g [⅓ cup] butter, softened and cut into cubes

50g [¼ cup] caster [granulated] sugar

1 large egg, beaten

½ tsp vanilla extract

3–4 Tbsp buttermilk

1 egg yolk, lightly beaten, for brushing

clotted cream, to serve

Berried Alive Syrup (makes 375ml [13fl oz])

1 Tbsp cornflour [cornstarch]

235ml [1 cup] water, plus 2 Tbsp

200g [2 cups] fresh blueberries

100g [½ cup] caster [superfine] sugar

Scones are dead easy to make. In fact, the hardest thing has been placing them in a category – they're neither cakes nor cookies, neither pastry nor bread, but hey, they have a raising agent, egg and butter so I'm calling them an enriched dough. Use the syrup to top 'ice screams', pancakes, waffles, yogurt… It also makes a lovely gift to give to friends and family.

Preheat the oven to 200°C fan [425°F/Gas mark 7] and line a baking tray with baking paper.

Sift the flour, baking powder and salt into a large bowl. Add the cubed butter and rub it in with your fingertips until the mixture looks like fine crumbs. Add the sugar, then make a well in the centre of your mix and add the egg and vanilla. Start mixing with your fingertips, then add the buttermilk, 1 Tbsp at a time, until you get a soft but not sticky dough.

Tip the dough onto a floured surface and bring it together, then roll it into a 2.5-cm [1-in] thick rectangle and cut out bats using a bat cookie cutter or a template.

Place the bats on the prepared baking tray and brush with the egg yolk to glaze. Bake for 10–12 minutes until risen and slightly golden. Let cool slightly.

Meanwhile, for the Berried Alive Syrup, mix the cornflour with the 2 Tbsp water in a bowl and set aside.

Add the blueberries, sugar and remaining water to a medium saucepan and bring to the boil. Reduce the heat and simmer for about 10 minutes, stirring occasionally. Add the cornflour mixture and stir. Let it thicken up a little, then remove the pan from heat. Divide the syrup into jars and chill in the fridge for up to 2 weeks.

Serve the warm scones with the syrup and clotted cream.

Brain Cinnamon Rolls

MAKES 4 LARGE BRAINS

180ml [¾ cup] whole milk

7-g [¼-oz] sachet of fast-action dried [active dry] yeast

55g [¼ cup] unsalted butter, melted, plus extra for greasing

50g [¼ cup] caster [granulated] sugar

1 large egg plus 1 egg yolk

red food colour

375g [3 cups] strong white bread flour, sifted, plus extra for dusting

½ tsp salt

½ quantity Cream Cheese Frosting (page 10) mixed with red food colour and a few drops of blue food colour

Filling

55g [¼ cup] unsalted butter, melted

110g [½ cup] dark brown sugar

1½ Tbsp ground cinnamon

I try not to be too gory in my bakes because, after all, it is food. However, one must sometimes break one's own rules. I desperately wanted to include my cinnamon roll recipe in this book and I felt that these brains were manageable for all baking levels. Don't be too put off, they are delicious!

Warm the milk in the microwave for about 20 seconds until lukewarm, then add it to a stand mixer fitted with a dough hook attachment. Sprinkle the yeast on top, add the melted butter, sugar, egg and egg yolk, then add enough red food colour to achieve a deep pink hue. Add the flour and salt and mix until everything is fully incorporated, then knead in the mixer for 5 minutes. The dough will be a little sticky. Cover the bowl with clingfilm [plastic wrap] or a clean towel and leave to rise in a warm place for 1½ hours, or until doubled in size.

Turn the risen dough out onto a floured surface and roll out to a 35 x 23-cm [14 x 9-in] wide rectangle. Brush with the melted butter for the filling.

Mix the brown sugar and cinnamon together. Use your hands to sprinkle the mixture over the buttered dough, then gently press into the butter a little. Tightly roll the dough up, starting from a shorter side, then place, seam side down, on the surface, making sure to seal the seam of the dough as best you can. Trim the edges and cut the roll into 8 equal pieces.

Grease 4 x 10-cm [4-in] round tins. Unroll the cinnamon roll (this seems stupid, but stay with me), then cut a straight piece and place in the middle of the prepared tins. Now zigzag the rest of that piece plus a second piece on either side. Cover and leave to rise for 45 minutes. Preheat the oven to 170°C fan [375°F/Gas mark 5].

Bake the cinnamon rolls for 20–25 minutes until golden, then leave to cool slightly. While still warm, brush with red cream cheese frosting and serve.

Pumpkin Brioche Buns

MAKES 8 BUNS

20ml [1½ Tbsp] whole milk, lukewarm (37°C [99°F])

7-g [¼-oz] sachet of fast-action dried [active dry] yeast

375g [3 cups] strong white bread flour, plus extra for dusting

1 tsp salt

4 eggs

75g [⅓ cup] caster [granulated] sugar

170g [¾ cup] butter, at room temperature

1 egg yolk, lightly beaten, for glazing

Brioche has to be my all-time favourite type of bread and had to be included in this book somehow. I normally make it using fresh yeast, but I know it isn't that easy to find, so I've adapted the recipe to be used with fast-action dried [active dry] yeast. The dough is quite sticky, but the result is delicious.

Place the warm milk in an electric mixer fitted with a dough hook attachment, then sprinkle in the yeast. Leave to rest for 3 minutes.

Add the flour, salt, eggs and sugar and knead for about 8 minutes. While the machine is kneading, add the butter, a little at a time. Cover with clingfilm [plastic wrap] or a clean towel and leave to rise in a warm place for 3 hours, or until doubled in size.

Knock back the dough, then place it on a lightly floured surface and divide it into 8 equal pieces.

Shape all the pieces into balls by rolling them and cupping them into the palm of your hand. Place on a baking tray lined with baking paper. Cover with a towel and leave to prove in a warm place for 1 hour, or until doubled in size.

Preheat the oven to 180°C fan [400°F/Gas mark 6].

Once the balls of dough have proved, score into 8 sections avoiding the middle so it doesn't split, then add a cashew nut in the middle for a 'stalk'.

Brush the pumpkins with the egg yolk and bake for 30 minutes, or until golden brown. Transfer to a wire rack to cool.

Pan de Muerto

MAKES 2 LOAVES

255ml [1 cup] whole milk

1 cinnamon stick

2 star anise

4 tsp fast-action dried [active dry] yeast

720g [5¾ cups] strong white bread flour, plus extra for dusting

3 large eggs

160g [⅔ cup] salted butter, softened

130g [⅔ cup] caster [granulated] sugar

1 egg yolk, lightly beaten, for glazing

icing [confectioners'] sugar, for dusting

Pan de muerto is a traditional bread from Mexico and it literally means 'bread of the dead'. It is usually baked in celebration of the Day of the Dead (All Saint's day in Spain). My version is a variation on the traditional, as it uses cinnamon and star anise to infuse the milk, and there's no orange.

Place the milk, cinnamon and star anise in a small saucepan over a medium heat and boil for 3 minutes to infuse the flavours. Leave to cool to lukewarm, about 35–39°C [95–102°F].

Remove the star anise and cinnamon stick from the milk and stir in the yeast. Leave to stand for 5 minutes.

Add the flour, eggs, softened butter and sugar to a stand mixer fitted with a dough hook attachment and start mixing, slowly adding the milk. Knead in the mixer for 3 minutes. Cover the bowl with clingfilm [plastic wrap] or a clean towel and leave to rise in a warm place for about 1 hour, or until doubled in size. Line a baking tray with baking paper.

Tip the dough out onto a lightly floured surface and knead it a couple of times to bring it together, then divide it into 2 equal pieces.

Take a little less than a third of the dough of each loaf and put it aside to create the bones. Shape the loaves of dough into balls and place on the prepared baking tray.

To make the bones, divide the reserved dough into 8 equal pieces, then shape each piece into a rope and snip both ends to create the bone shape. Place 4 bones around each loaf, cover and leave to rise again for 1 hour.

Preheat the oven to 170°C [375°F/Gas mark 5]. Brush the bread with the egg yolk and bake for 40–45 minutes until golden brown. Transfer to a wire rack to cool, then sprinkle with icing sugar.

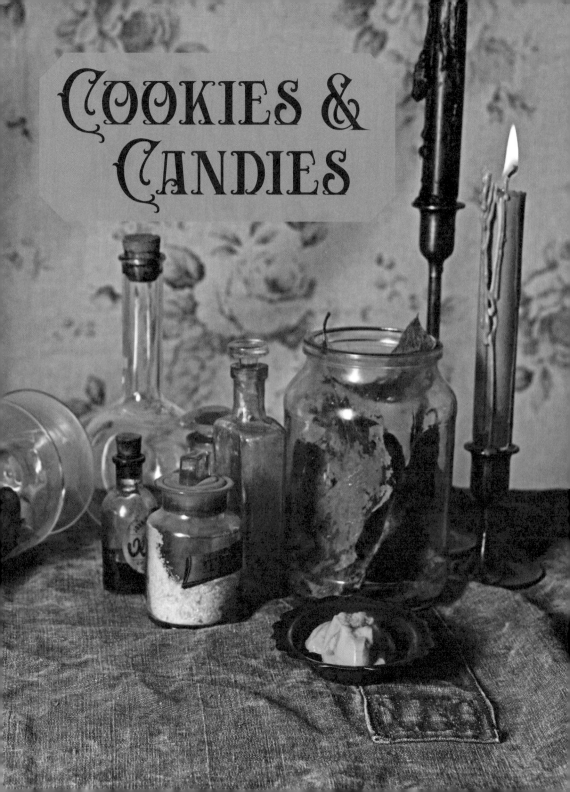

COOKIES & CANDIES

Autopsy Frogs

MAKES 8-10 FROGS

leaf green food colour

150g [5oz] green Candy Melts

1 Tbsp butter

75g [2 cups] mini marshmallows

1½ Tbsp red velvet cake mix

½ tsp vanilla extract

red food colour

50g [2 cups] Rice Krispies

Inspired by Honeydukes' peppermint toads but with a rather gory interior, I guess this is my take on chocolate Rice Krispies treats. How much will your kid love you if you add one of these to his or her lunch box? I can't wait until I can do that with my daughter.

Brush the frog mould with a little leaf green food colour to create darker areas around the frogs' bodies.

Melt the Candy Melts in a heatproof bowl set over a saucepan of gently simmering water, making sure the base of the bowl doesn't touch the water. Alternatively, melt in a microwave at 30-second intervals. Pour a thin layer into the mould – it helps to use a brush to spread it evenly. Refrigerate while making the 'guts'.

Melt the butter in a medium saucepan on low heat, add the marshmallows and stir until fully melted. Remove from the heat and mix in the velvet cake mix, vanilla and enough red food colour to achieve a strong red. Return the pan to the heat if the mixture starts to harden. Stir in the Rice Krispies and mix until fully incorporated.

Remove the mould from the refrigerator and fill each frog with the Rice Krispie mixture. Press the filling down firmly and smooth the top.

If the remaining Candy Melts have reset, melt them again and use to cover the bases of the frogs, smoothing out neatly. Refrigerate for 20 minutes, then unmould. Eat within 4 days.

Tip: you can buy frog mould trays online, especially in Harry Potter themes!

* Photographed on previous spread

Gingerdead Twins

MAKES 12 GINGERDEAD TWINS

450g [3½ cups] plain [all-purpose] flour, plus extra for dusting

½ tsp salt

1 Tbsp ground ginger

1¾ tsp ground cinnamon

¼ tsp ground cloves

80g [6 Tbsp] unsalted butter, at room temperature

165g [¾ cup] dark brown sugar

1 large egg

230g [⅔ cup] golden [light corn] syrup, maple syrup or molasses

2 tsp vanilla extract

Royal icing
3 egg whites

1 tsp vanilla extract

600g [5 cups] icing [confectioners'] sugar, sifted

To decorate
blue food colour

pink food colour

cocoa powder

black edible ink pen

red edible ink pen

green edible ink pen

red powder food colour

Although inspired by the creepy twins from the 1980s horror film *The Shining*, these cookies still maintain the classic gingerbread features. Draw the silhouette of the twins on a piece of paper and use it as a template. If you don't feel confident icing them with royal icing, you can always cut the dress out of modelling chocolate or fondant and decorate that, but if I'm able to do it, you can too, as I hardly ever ice cookies!

Sift the flour, salt and spices into a large bowl. Set aside.

Mix the butter, brown sugar and egg together in another bowl. I like to use a wooden spoon for this – somehow gingerbread seems like it has to be mixed with a wooden spoon. Add the syrup and vanilla and continue to mix.

Mix in the dry ingredients and combine until smooth.

Divide the dough in half and wrap in clingfilm [plastic wrap] pressing down to create 2 discs. Refrigerate for 3 hours, or up to 3 days.

Preheat the oven to 180°C fan [400°F/Gas mark 6] and line a baking tray with baking paper.

Roll out the first disc of dough on a lightly floured surface to about 5mm [¼in] thick. Cut out 6 cookies by cutting around your template (see introduction) with a small sharp knife and place on a lined baking tray.

Bake for 7–10 minutes – the longer they are in the oven, the snappier they will be, but I like them a bit soft. Leave to cool completely on a wire rack before icing.

Repeat with the second disc of dough to make 6 more cookies or alternatively, freeze for another time.

cont...

For the royal icing, whisk the egg whites until frothy, then stir in the vanilla extract. Slowly add the icing sugar, mixing until fully incorporated. If the mixture is too thick, add a little water. If it is too thin, add more icing sugar, 1 Tbsp at a time.

Dye small amounts of the icing pink and blue with food colouring, and a third amount brown with the cocoa powder. Decorate each twin by outlining the dress with piped blue royal icing, then filling in the outline. Pipe the little lace details with white icing around the hem of the sleeves, collar and skirt hem. Leave to dry, then pipe on the pink belt and buttons, and the brown hair.

Pipe the eyes in white and draw the eye lashes with the black edible ink pen. Draw the mouth with the red edible ink pen and finish the faces with a dust of red coloured powder on the cheeks.

Leave to dry completely before adding the lace on the belt with white icing, the shoes with black pen, and green irises and black dots on the eyeballs.

The gingerbread twins will keep in an airtight container for around 2 weeks.

Tip: I made and decorated a gingerbread board to display the twins, but if you're eating or storing yours straightaway, you don't need to make one of these.

Monster Fortune Cookies

MAKES 16 COOKIES

2 large egg whites

100g [½ cup] caster [superfine] sugar

45g [3 Tbsp] butter, melted

½ tsp vanilla extract

¼ tsp almond extract

2 tsp water

100g [¾ cup] plain [all-purpose] flour

2 tsp cornflour [cornstarch]

pinch of salt

⅓ quantity Royal Icing (page 81–2), to decorate

I had never felt the need to make fortune cookies until I saw them as gruesome monsters desperate to deliver a macabre message. My husband and I love to cook Chinese food for dinner parties, so I thought it would be great fun to provide our friends with these treats at the end of our meal. They are also perfect for a Chinese New Year party.

Preheat the oven to 170°C fan [375°F/Gas mark 5] and line a baking tray with a silicone mat or baking paper.

Whisk the egg whites and sugar in a stand mixer fitted with a whisk attachment on high speed until frothy. Add the butter, vanilla and almond extracts and the water and continue mixing until combined.

Sift both flours into a bowl and add the salt. Add it to the egg mixture and mix until smooth.

Spoon 1 Tbsp of batter onto the prepared tray and spread it thinly with the bottom of your spoon to form a 7.5-cm [3-in] circle. You will need to bake them in batches of 2 or 3 as they cool very quickly and need shaping. Bake for 7–9 minutes until the edges start to brown.

Roll 2–3 balls of foil. When the cookies are ready, remove them from the oven. Place a foil ball in the centre of a cookie circle to stop the mouth closing completely, then flip one side over to make a semi-circle and press the edges together to seal on either side of the foil. Carefully remove the foil ball. Place the shaped cookies in a muffin tin so they hold their shape and repeat to cook and shape the remaining batter.

Cut a piece of paper into strips and cut a snake tongue end, then write a macabre message on with a pen. Stick the paper 'tongue' into the cookie with a little royal icing. Fill a small piping bag with the remaining royal icing and, using a very small nozzle, pipe little fangs.

Maple Bat Cookies

MAKES ABOUT 24

170g [¾ cup] unsalted butter, at room temperature

90ml [⅓ cup] maple syrup

50g [¼ cup] light brown sugar

200g [1½ cups] plain [all-purpose] flour, plus extra for dusting

1 Tbsp cornflour [cornstarch]

¼ tsp salt

Hot Maple Milk (page 111), to serve

To decorate

⅓ quantity Royal Icing (page 81–2)

black sanding sugar

red food colour

I came back from a recent trip to Canada full of ideas for maple-flavoured goodies. These cheeky bat cookies were one of the first things I tried and I was so pleased with the result – crispy and buttery with a wonderful maple flavour. Make a little rectangular slit in the bottom of some of them so they can sit on the rim of your favourite teacup, but be careful – these bats can quickly fly away.

Beat the butter, maple syrup and brown sugar together in an electric mixer until light and fluffy.

Mix the flours and salt together in a bowl with a fork. Add the dry ingredients to the butter mixture and mix until fully incorporated, making sure to scrape the sides and base of the bowl. Cover with clingfilm [plastic wrap] and refrigerate for 1 hour. I sometimes leave it overnight.

Preheat the oven to 170°C fan [375°F/Gas mark 5] and line a baking tray with baking paper.

Roll the dough out on a floured surface and cut out shapes using a bat cookie cutter or a template. Place on the prepared baking tray and bake for 12–14 minutes until the edges start to brown. Leave to cool on a wire rack.

Brush some royal icing on the wings and sprinkle with the black sanding sugar.

Colour some royal icing red. Dip a cocktail stick [toothpick] in the red icing and dot onto the cookie for the eyes, dragging the stick up to create a point. Repeat with uncoloured icing for the fangs, this time dragging the stick down.

Leave to set, then serve with a cup of Hot Maple Milk. Eat the cookies within 4 days.

'Eye Love You' Truffles

MAKES ABOUT 20 TRUFFLES

20 Oreo cookies

60g [¼ cup] mascarpone cheese

60g [¼ cup] cream cheese

pinch of salt

175g [6oz] white chocolate, melted

To decorate
green food colour

black edible paint

black edible ink pen

red edible ink pen

What better way to say 'eye love you' than with an edible handmade gift? These truffles are so delicious and very easy to make. I have presented them in an edible chocolate box. I found the mould online and made the base out of dark chocolate, the lid with red and pink Candy Melts and added a little eye on top. Whichever way you present these truffles, I guarantee they will be a hit.

Pulse the Oreos in a food processor until you have a fine crumb consistency. Add the mascarpone, cream cheese and salt and continue pulsing until a sticky paste forms.

Line a baking tray with baking paper. Roll the mixture into 2-cm [¾-in] diameter balls, then place on the prepared tray and freeze for 30 minutes.

Dip each truffle into the melted white chocolate, then place them back on the tray and chill in the fridge for about 20 minutes until set.

Once set, paint the eye using the green food colour for the iris and the black paint for the pupil. Add lines to the iris with the black pen. Make them bloodshot by drawing veins with the red pen.

Meese's Pieces

50g [1¾oz] white chocolate, broken into pieces

50g [1¾oz] pink Candy Melts

vegetable oil (optional)

150g [5oz] milk or dark chocolate, broken into pieces

130g [½ cup] smooth peanut butter

3 Tbsp icing [confectioners'] sugar, sifted

8 pieces of string, each about 6cm [2½in] long

I absolutely love peanut butter cups, but they have only recently appeared in the UK. This is why I created my own version a while back, giving them a rather contemporary take. Imagine a marital union between a sugar mouse and a peanut butter cup: these meese's pieces would be their offspring.

Melt the white chocolate and pink Candy Melts in 2 separate small heatproof bowls set over saucepans of gently simmering water, making sure the bases of the bowls don't touch the water. Alternatively, melt in a microwave at 30-second intervals. Sometimes the Candy Melts don't melt smoothly, but you can add some vegetable oil to thin them, if needed.

Using a teaspoon, drizzle some white chocolate in a zigzag motion over the mice mould, then repeat with the pink Candy Melts. Refrigerate for 5 minutes while you melt the dark or milk chocolate.

Once the drizzles have set, spoon a thin layer of the melted dark or milk chocolate into the mould and use a brush to spread it so it evenly coats the mould. Make sure you save enough chocolate to seal the mice once filled. Refrigerate for 20 minutes.

Mix the peanut butter and icing sugar together in a small bowl until fully incorporated.

Remove the moulds from the refrigerator and fill with the peanut butter mixture, then stick on the string tails.

Remelt the leftover chocolate and cover the peanut butter mixture with a thin layer. Refrigerate for another 15 minutes, or until fully set. Eat within 4 days.

Tip: you can buy moulds for sugar mice online.

All Saints Lollipops

MAKES 8-10 LARGE LOLLIPOPS

400g [2 cups] granulated sugar

225g [⅔ cup] liquid glucose or light corn syrup

60ml [¼ cup] water

2 tsp flavour extract (I've used blackberry)

black or purple food colour

200g [7oz] white candy floss [cotton candy]

ribbon, to decorate (optional)

Don't tell me these aren't the cutest sugar-coated little ghosts. They are just perfect to give as presents, but I also think they make a fantastic 'Witchmas' tree decoration. The colour and flavour combinations are totally up to you, but it makes sense to colour them dark, so the eyes and mouth stand out against the fluffy exterior. You will need 8–10 lollipop sticks and a sugar thermometer.

Line 1–2 large baking trays with a silicone mat or baking paper and place 8–10 lollipop [popsicle] sticks about 10cm [4in] apart from each other.

Have a large bowl of iced water ready nearby. In a medium saucepan, combine the sugar, liquid glucose and water over a medium-high heat and stir until the sugar dissolves.

Insert a sugar thermometer, bring the mixture to the boil and boil until it reaches 154°C [309°F] or hard ball stage, making sure to brush down the sugar crystals forming on the sides of the pan with a wet pastry brush. Do not stir while it's boiling. Once it reaches that temperature, quickly place the pan in the iced water to avoid caramelization.

Remove the pan from the bowl once it stops bubbling, and add the flavour extract and food colour.

Pour the mixture over each stick in an oval shape, then leave them to cool at room temperature for 30 minutes.

Wrap each lollipop in candy floss, shaping it into a point at the top. Wet your finger and poke a hole for the eyes and mouths. Decorate with ribbon, if you like.

Creepmas Wreath Cookies

MAKES 36 COOKIES

225g [1 cup] salted butter

190g [1½ cups icing [confectioners'] sugar, plus extra for dusting

1 large egg

1 tsp vanilla extract

½ tsp almond extract

juniper green or leaf green food colour (optional)

300g [2¼ cups] plain [all-purpose] flour, sifted, plus extra for dusting

1 tsp bicarbonate of soda [baking soda]

1 tsp cream of tartar

To decorate
Buttercream (page 34) or Royal Icing (page 81–2)

juniper green food colour

72 yellow Smarties

sugarpaste or white modelling chocolate for the teeth

black gel food colour

holly and berries sprinkles (optional)

red ribbon (optional)

I posted these cookies online last Christmas and they got such an incredible reception that I thought I must include them in this book. They are inspired by the movie *The Nightmare Before Christmas*, but by adding a pretty red bow and some little berry sprinkles, they somehow seem a little less scary. They can easily be turned into Christmas tree decorations by poking a hole through the top before baking and threading some ribbon through to hang them up.

Cream the butter and sugar together in an electric mixer until light and fluffy. Add the egg, vanilla and almond extracts and enough food colour to turn the dough green, if you like. Mix to combine but do not overmix. Add the flour, bicarbonate of soda and cream of tartar and mix until combined.

Divide the dough in half, cover each portion in clingfilm [plastic wrap] and refrigerate for at least 2 hours.

Preheat the oven to 170°C fan [375°F/Gas mark 5] and line a baking tray with baking paper.

Roll out one half of the dough on a lightly floured surface to about 4mm [⅛in] thickness. Cut out 18 circles using a round 8.5-cm [3⅓-in] cookie cutter then use a 4-cm [1½-in] cutter to cut out inner circles to make wreaths.

Place the cookies on the prepared baking tray and bake for 7–9 minutes until the edges start to brown.

Leave them to cool slightly on the baking tray before transferring them to a wire rack to cool completely.

cont...

Colour your buttercream or royal icing green and place in a piping [pastry] bag with a small leaf tip. If you don't have that tip, just cut a small 'V' shape at the bottom of the piping bag.

To decorate your cookies, start by sticking the Smartie eyes on with a little buttercream or icing so they stick, then pipe the eyelids over the top and bottom of the eyes.

For the leaves, starting at the outer edge of the wreath, pipe little leaves all around the wreath and around the eyes. Continue to fill the entire wreath.

To make the teeth, mould them out of your chosen ingredient by rolling a small ball in the palm of your hand and pressing on one side to achieve a pointy end. Bend them slightly like a claw and attach them with a little buttercream or icing.

Paint 2 black little dots in the middle of the eyes with gel food colour and sprinkle the wreath with some berries and holly leaf sprinkles, if using. Dust with a little icing sugar and add a ribbon bow, if you like. Eat within 3 days.

Repeat the process with the other half of the dough, although I tend to freeze it for a later date.

Vampire Macarons

MAKES 40 MACARONS

200g [7oz] ground almonds

200g [7oz] icing [confectioners']
sugar

160g [5½oz] egg whites,
at room temperature

¼ tsp cream of tartar

45g [1½oz] water

175g [6oz] caster [superfine]
sugar

blue and purple food colours

Dark chocolate ganache filling
300g [10½oz] dark chocolate
chips

150g [5¼oz] double [heavy]
cream

1 tsp black gel food colour

To decorate
black food paint

white food paint or edible ink
pen

red powder food colour

Macarons are a little tricky to get right, but after years of using the French method, I swapped to the Italian one and it's never failed me. Still, you may find they don't quite work out for you straightaway, but don't be disheartened, just give them another go! You need to use kitchen scales not cup measurements for this recipe as it needs to be precise on weight. Get creative with your vampire faces – this is an opportunity to give each one individuality. You will need a sugar thermometer for this recipe.

Line 2 baking trays with silicone mats or baking paper.

Put the ground almonds and icing sugar in a food processor and pulse a few times to grind it finer. Sift the mixture into a large bowl and combine with 80g [2¾oz] of the egg whites. Set aside.

Pour the remaining egg whites into a stand mixer fitted with a whisk attachment and add the cream of tartar. Don't turn it on yet.

Heat the water and caster sugar together in a small saucepan over a medium heat and stir until the sugar has dissolved. Insert the sugar thermometer and when it reaches 110°C [230°F], start whisking the egg whites on low-medium speed until thick and glossy.

Once the thermometer reaches 118°C [244°F], start pouring the syrup slowly into the meringue. Whisk for 8–10 minutes until the mixture cools down. When you touch the bowl, it should still feel warm.

Add the food colour (I mix purple with a little blue to get that dead vampire glow) then pour the meringue into the almond mixture and fold in with a spatula until it is shiny and a lava-like consistency.

cont...

Pour the macaron batter into a piping [pastry] bag with a large round nozzle and pipe about neat circles about 2.5cm [1in] wide onto the prepared trays. You should get about 80.

Rap the trays on the work surface 6–8 times to remove any air bubbles. If any smaller bubbles remain, pop them with a pin or toothpick.

Let the macarons rest for 45 minutes or so to form a skin. Once they have formed a skin you should be able to touch them gently without getting batter on your finger.

Meanwhile, preheat the oven to 160°C fan [350°F/Gas mark 4].

Bake the macarons for 12–14 minutes until they are dry and firm. Leave to cool on a wire rack.

For the ganache, place the chocolate chips in a heatproof bowl. Bring the cream to just before boiling point in a saucepan, then pour it over the chocolate chips and allow them to melt. Mix well, then add the black food colour. Spoon into a piping bag with a star nozzle, pipe onto a macaron shell and sandwich together with another. Repeat to sandwich all the macarons with ganache.

Once your macaron shells are all paired up and filled, draw and paint their faces. Paint the hair, eyes and mouths with black food paint, the fangs with white food paint and the rosy cheeks with the red powder.

Ghost and Bat Jelly Sweets

MAKES 500G [1LB 2OZ]

3 x 12g packets (total 1¼oz) powdered gelatine

280ml [1¼ cups] water

400g [2 cups] granulated sugar

black food colour, for the bats

½ tsp cherry extract, or whatever flavour you prefer

½ tsp coconut extract, or whatever flavour you prefer

non-stick baking spray

100g [½ cup] caster [granulated] sugar

1 Tbsp citric acid

I can't recommend making your own sweets [candies] enough – it's like creating kitchen alchemy and the smell in the house afterwards is just divine. They are the perfect thing to make to give to trick or treaters, or to gift to friends and family. The flavour and shape combinations are endless. They need to set for about 8 hours, so it makes sense to make them the night before. I bought the silicone moulds very cheaply online, but you can use whatever you like (skulls, for example) – just make sure the mould isn't too intricate as it will be hard to get the sweets out – they are sticky.

Sprinkle the gelatine over 100ml [½ cup] of the water in a large saucepan (the mixture will bubble so make sure the pan is large) and let it bloom for 5 minutes.

Bring the remaining water to the boil in another saucepan, add the granulated sugar and stir until fully dissolved. Pour into the gelatine pan and stir until completely dissolved, then simmer on low heat for 5 minutes.

Divide the mixture between 2 glass measuring jars, add the black food colour and a few drops of the cherry extract into one, and the coconut extract into the other and mix both jars well.

Spray your silicone moulds with non-stick spray and pour the mixture in carefully. Refrigerate overnight until set.

The next day, mix the caster sugar and citric acid together in a shallow bowl. Remove the jelly sweets from the mould and roll in the sugar until fully coated. Eat within 2–3 weeks.

Baked Marzipan Mistle-toes

MAKES 20 TOES

200g [2 cups] ground almonds

200g [1½ cups minus 1 Tbsp] icing [confectioners'] sugar

1 egg, separated

green food colour

This recipe originated in Toledo in Spain and is most likely of Arabic origin. The marzipan is traditionally shaped like seashells, bows or fish and served at Christmas. For the best results, you need to blanch, peel and grind the almonds, but just use ground almonds if you are not in the mood for boiling nuts! The marzipan figures, in this case toes, are baked for a few minutes to give them a golden finish.

Pour the ground almonds and icing sugar into a food processor and pulse a few times to grind the almonds further. Add the egg white, then pulse until the mixture comes together.

Reserve a little uncoloured marzipan to use as nails and berries, then add the green colour to the rest and mix in until incorporated.

Tip the green marzipan out onto a clean surface and knead it with your hands. If the mixture feels too dry, add a little water, and if it's too sticky, add more ground almonds. Bring together into a ball, wrap in clingfilm [plastic wrap] and leave to rest in a dry place for 1 hour.

Preheat the oven to 180°C fan [400°F/Gas mark 6] and line a baking tray with baking paper.

Break off little pieces of marzipan and form into balls. To shape into a toe, mould with your hands into a toe shape, then using your thumb, press the area where the nail will be. Roll out the white marzipan and cut out the nails, then place them on the toes.

Score wrinkles with a sharp knife or scalpel. I've added some warts to some of them too. Use any leftover marzipan to make leaves and berries to decorate.

Brush with the egg yolk and bake for 5 minutes, or until slightly golden. Serve on the ends of skewers, tied with a ribbon, if you like.

Dragon Scream Eggs

MAKES 2 LARGE EGGS

115g [½ cup] whipping cream

140g [⅔ cup] cream cheese, at room temperature

3 Tbsp icing [confectioners'] sugar, sifted

1 tsp vanilla extract

finely grated zest of 1 clementine

250g [9oz] chocolate buttons

2 hollow chocolate Easter eggs

metallic powder food colours (optional)

Orange curd
2 large egg yolks

75g [6 Tbsp] caster [superfine] sugar

finely grated zest and juice of 1 small clementine

1 heaped Tbsp cold butter

Breakfast is served! What an Easter morning treat this is – chocolate dragon eggs filled with delicious cheesecake mousse and an orange curd 'yolk'. If you feel like going all out, make edible spoons by simply baking shortbread/sugar cookie dough in spoon moulds. Serve in little ceramic egg cups.

To make the cream cheese mousse, whip the cream to form soft peaks. In a separate bowl, mix the cream cheese, icing sugar, vanilla and the clementine zest together with a spatula until light and fluffy. Fold in the whipped cream and chill in the fridge for 1 hour.

For the orange curd, whisk the egg yolks and caster sugar together in a heatproof bowl set over a pan of gently simmering water, making sure the base of the bowl doesn't touch the water. Add the clementine zest and juice and continue whisking until the curd coats the back of a wooden spoon. Remove from the heat and add the cold butter. Mix well and leave to cool.

Melt a handful of the chocolate buttons in a microwaveable bowl at 20-second intervals in the microwave, then pour into a piping [pastry] bag. This will be used for gluing the scales onto the eggshells.

Crack the tops of the chocolate eggs open. Place the eggs in egg cups and, starting from just above the cup, attach the remaining chocolate buttons in rows, overlapping them as they go up. Brush the eggs with metallic powder, if you like.

Spoon or pipe the cheesecake mousse inside the Easter eggs, to fill them three-quarters full, then add a dollop of curd to imitate a yolk. Voilà!

Pumpkin and Pecan Cookies

MAKES 24

125g [¾ cup] shelled pecans, chopped

2 Tbsp salted butter, melted

170g [¾ cup] unsalted butter, softened

170g [¾ cup] light brown sugar

200g [1 cup] pumpkin purée

2 tsp vanilla extract

1 egg

260g [2 cups] plain [all-purpose] flour

1 tsp bicarbonate of soda [baking soda]

1 tsp ground cinnamon

1 tsp ground nutmeg

pinch of ground cloves

½ tsp salt

Pumpkin and pecan are two of my most favourite flavours. These cookies are a mixture of pumpkin pie and pecan butter cookies and are the perfect accompaniment for a Pumpkin Spice Latte (see page 115) on a rainy afternoon.

Preheat the oven to 170°C fan [375°F/Gas mark 5] and line a baking tray with baking paper.

Coat the pecans with the melted butter in a bowl. Spread out on the prepared baking tray and bake for 5–7 minutes until they start to toast. Leave to cool. Keep the oven on.

Cream the softened butter and sugar together in an electric mixer until light and fluffy. Add the pumpkin purée, vanilla and egg and continue mixing.

Sift the flour, bicarbonate of soda, spices and salt into a separate bowl, then slowly add it to the wet ingredients. Add the cooled pecans and mix to form a dough.

Form balls of around 2 Tbsp of dough and place them on a baking tray lined with baking paper. Bake for 10–12 minutes. They will look slightly undercooked when you take them out, but they will harden a little as they cool. Transfer to a wire rack to cool and eat within 4 days.

Drinks & Desserts

Midnight Flight Cocktail

MAKES 600ML [20FL OZ]
VIOLET SYRUP AND
1 COCKTAIL

Violet syrup
4–5 large handfuls of violet heads, petals only

235ml [1 cup] boiling water

400g [2 cups] caster [granulated] sugar

Cocktail
40ml [1½oz] gin

20ml [¾fl oz] fresh lemon juice

1½ Tbsp violet syrup

crushed ice

sparkling wine, chilled, to top up

To garnish
sugared violets

dry ice (optional)

Despite the name of this cocktail, I'm not encouraging you to drink and fly, so leave the broomstick securely parked in your cupboard. First, you will need to make the violet syrup, which can be made by boiling the violets in sugared water. It's also available to buy, but there's something special about making floral syrups, especially if you have picked the ingredients from the wild. Bottle the violet syrup and use it to flavour buttercreams, icings [frostings] or drinks.

If you are making the violet syrup, make it at least a day in advance. Sterilize the bottle you are using to store it in by washing the bottle in hot, soapy water, rinsing and drying it out in an oven preheated to 120°C fan [275°F/Gas mark 1].

Place the flower petals in a heatproof bowl and pour over the boiling water. Cover and leave to stand at room temperature for 12–24 hours.

The next day, add the sugar to the violets and water, then set the bowl over a saucepan of gently simmering water, making sure the water doesn't touch the base of the bowl. Cook, stirring constantly, until the sugar dissolves.

Strain the mixture through a sieve and bottle. I keep mine in the refrigerator for up to 10 months, when it starts to lose its colour.

To make the cocktail, add the gin, lemon juice and violet syrup to a cocktail shaker filled with crushed ice. Shake and strain into a chilled glass. Top with sparkling wine and garnish with sugared violets. Add a little piece of dry ice for an extra witchy touch.

* Photographed on previous pages

Hot Maple Milk

480ml [2 cups] semi-skimmed milk

460ml [2 cups] single [light] cream

160ml [½ cup] maple syrup

1 tsp vanilla extract

pinch of freshly grated nutmeg, plus extra to garnish

This is the perfect transitional drink from autumn to winter. It really is delicious and so easy to make. I've never tried this, but I imagine it can be easily spiked with some brandy or whisky for a more celebratory feel. The Maple Bat Cookies on page 87 are the perfect accompaniment for this drink.

Combine the milk, cream, maple syrup, vanilla and a pinch of nutmeg in a saucepan over a low-medium heat. Stir and warm the mixture without letting it boil.

Divide between 6 mugs and sprinkle with freshly grated nutmeg.

* Photographed on page 86

Vampire Blood Punch

SERVES 8-10

2 litres [8½ cups] cranberry juice

75ml [⅓ cup] fresh orange juice

200ml [¾ cup plus 1 Tbsp] lemon-lime flavour soda

2 Tbsp caster [granulated] sugar

red food colour (optional)

black sanding sugar, to decorate

vampire gummy teeth, to decorate

I tend to write recipes for alcohol-free drinks so all ages can enjoy them, and then suggest a way to make the drink alcoholic. In this case, vodka would be the alcohol of choice. Add it to taste, if you like. Another tip for this punch is to pour the mixture into an ice-cube tray (bat ice cubes ideally), freeze, then add them to the punch bowl. This way, the punch will stay cold and full of flavour.

Mix all the ingredients together well in a punch bowl. Add ice and serve cold with sanding sugar around the rim of each glass and vampire gummy teeth attached to it.

Poison Hot Apple Drink

SERVES 12-14

2 litres [8½ cups] [hard] apple cider

500ml [2 cups] pineapple juice

2 cinnamon sticks, plus extra to serve

This is a different type of autumnal taste explosion, and is much easier to make than mulled cider. It is the perfect drink to serve at either a Halloween or Christmas party. Leave it on the stove at the lowest setting possible and let your guests serve themselves.

Add all the ingredients to a large pot (or cauldron) and simmer for about 1 hour. Serve warm with a cinnamon stick.

Pumpkin Spice Latte

Pumpkin spice mix
5–6 whole cloves

2 tsp ground cinnamon

1 tsp ground ginger

½ tsp ground nutmeg

Latte
1 tsp maple syrup

¼ tsp pumpkin spice mix

80ml [⅓ cup] hot, strong brewed coffee

120ml [½ cup] warm milk

whipped cream, to serve (optional)

Pumpkin spice is not available already made in the UK, but it is very simple to make. Once all the spices are mixed together, making your latte takes seconds and it is so much nicer than the ones available in the shops. Also, you don't need to wait for autumn to enjoy this!

Grind the cloves in a mortar and pestle until ground. Transfer to a small bowl and mix in the rest of the spices. You can double or triple the amounts and store in an airtight container.

To make the latte, add the maple syrup to a cup and stir in the spice mix. Add the coffee and warm milk and stir well. Top with whipped cream, if you like.

Scary Berry Ice Cream

SERVES 4

450g [1lb] green gooseberries, rinsed, plus extra to decorate

1 Tbsp water

115g [generous ½ cup] caster [granulated] sugar

120ml [½ cup] double [heavy] cream

green food colour

2 Tbsp milk or dark chocolate chips, melted

black edible ink pen

This is my take on a retro dessert that uses gooseberries. Gooseberries are in season in summertime, so this is definitely a summer dessert. Draw various Jack O'Lantern designs on fresh gooseberries for decoration or use dried ones for shrunken heads. Serve in old-fashioned ice cream bowls or glasses. Charity shops [thrift stores] are a great place to find these.

Place the gooseberries, water and sugar in a saucepan over a low-medium heat and simmer for about 15 minutes, or until the berries have broken down completely.

Transfer the mixture to a food processor and whizz until puréed. Rub the fruit mixture through a fine sieve, discarding the skins and pips, and leave to cool completely.

If using an ice-cream maker, pour the mixture into the machine with the unwhipped cream and food colour and churn following the manufacturer's instructions.

If not using a machine, whip the cream until stiff peaks form, then add the gooseberry purée and food colour and fold to combine. Pour the mixture into a shallow freezerproof container and freeze for 2 hours, or until partially frozen.

Pour the semi-frozen mixture into a chilled bowl and whisk until creamy and smooth, then return to the freezer and freeze until firm, about 4 hours or overnight.

Serve the ice cream with a dollop of melted chocolate on top and decorated with scary berries – gooseberries with Jack O'Lantern faces drawn on with an edible black pen or dried ones as shrunken heads or ghosts.

Cherry and White Chocolate Eye Domes

MAKES 12 DOMES

150g [5¼oz] fresh cherries, pitted

juice of ½ lemon

75g [⅓ cup] caster [granulated] sugar

150g [5¼oz] white chocolate, broken into pieces

210ml [1 cup minus 1 Tbsp] whipping cream

150g [⅔ cup] full-fat cream cheese

190g [¾ cup plus 1 Tbsp] mascarpone cheese

45g [5 Tbsp] icing [confectioners'] sugar, sifted

1 tsp vanilla extract

To decorate
150g [5oz] white modelling chocolate or sugarpaste

green food colour

black edible ink pen

white edible paint

red edible ink pen

powder food colours of your choice for petals

leaf veiner (optional)

50ml [1¾fl oz] clear piping gel

These domes are inspired by the talking flowers in *Alice's Adventures in Wonderland*, but with a creepy rather than cute look. If you decide to give this dessert a go, you would have made a classic 'pâtisserie' dessert, so pat yourself on the back. These domes can be placed on top of tarts, or they can be served on top of pastry leaves, or just as they are. You will need semi-sphere silicone moulds roughly 8cm [3in] in diameter and a sugar thermometer. You can also halve the recipe if you are serving fewer people.

Blitz the pitted cherries, lemon juice and caster sugar together in a food processor until smooth. Pour into a small saucepan and bring to the boil. Reduce the heat and simmer for 4–5 minutes until it thickens, stirring so it doesn't stick to the base of the pan. Leave to cool.

Melt the white chocolate in a heatproof bowl set over a pan of gently simmering water, making sure the base of the bowl doesn't touch the water. Remove from the pan and leave to cool to room temperature.

Beat the cream in a separate bowl with a handheld electric whisk until soft peaks form.

Whisk both cheeses, the icing sugar and vanilla together in another bowl until combined. Add the whipped cream to the cream cheese mixture, then add the melted white chocolate and mix until combined.

Divide the filling equally between 2 bowls, then mix about 75g [2¾oz] of the cherry mixture into one of the bowls.

cont...

Add about 1 Tbsp of the white cheesecake mixture into each semi-sphere mould, then add 1 tsp of the cherry mixture, then 1 Tbsp of the cherry cheesecake mixture and finish with another layer of white cheesecake mixture. Smooth the tops with a palette knife and freeze overnight.

To make the eyeballs, divide some of the modelling chocolate into 12 equal balls, about 1.5cm [⅝in] in diameter. Paint the eyes using green food colour for the irises. Leave to dry, then draw on the pupil with the black pen and the fine lines coming off it. Dab a little white for reflection with edible paint. Make the eyes bloodshot by drawing veins with the red ink pen. Set aside.

Roll the rest of the modelling chocolate out on baking paper until it is 2mm [1⁄16in] thick. Cut out petals and colour them using the powder colours. Alternatively, you can use a silicone mould to create the petal's veins by simply pressing a little ball of sugarpaste between the 2 parts of the veiner.

Take the domes out of the freezer and unmould them. Scoop out a bit off the curved top in order to place the eyeball in. Add the petals starting from the top and overlapping them. Finally, brush some piping gel onto the eyeballs to give them a real glazed appearance.

Fly Agaric Dome Desserts

MAKES 12 FLY AGARICS

150g [5¼oz] fresh cherries, pitted

juice of ½ lemon

75g [⅓ cup] caster [granulated] sugar

150g [5¼oz] white chocolate, broken into pieces

210ml [1 cup minus 1 Tbsp] whipping cream

150g [⅔ cup] full-fat cream cheese

190g [¾ cup plus 1 Tbsp] mascarpone cheese

45g [5 Tbsp] icing [confectioners'] sugar, sifted

1 tsp vanilla extract

Mirror glaze
5 gelatine leaves

150g [¾ cup plus 2 tsp] white chocolate chips

150ml [⅔ cup] liquid glucose

150g [¾ cup] caster [granulated] sugar

70ml [4½ Tbsp] water

100g [⅓ cup] condensed milk

red food colour

desiccated coconut, for sprinkling

Meringue stalks
2 large egg whites

2 Tbsp caster [superfine] sugar

These are a variation of the Cherry and White Chocolate Eye Domes (page 118). They are slightly less time-consuming but just as tasty. These domes have the same flavour as the eye domes, but they have a mirror glaze on top and the stalks are made out of meringue. I am an avid mushroom forager and no matter how many times I come across this iconic fly agaric mushroom, it never ceases to make me smile. Eating this version of the *Amanita muscaria* will be less eventful for sure. You will need semi-sphere silicone moulds roughly 8cm [3in] in diameter and a sugar thermometer.

Blitz the pitted cherries, lemon juice and caster sugar together in a food processor until smooth. Pour into a small saucepan and bring to the boil. Reduce the heat and simmer for 4–5 minutes until it thickens, stirring constantly, so it doesn't stick to the base of the pan. Leave to cool.

Melt the white chocolate in a heatproof bowl set over a pan of gently simmering water, making sure the base of the bowl doesn't touch the water. Remove from the pan and leave to cool to room temperature.

Beat the cream in a separate bowl with a handheld electric whisk until soft peaks form.

Whisk both cheeses, the icing sugar and vanilla together in another bowl until combined. Add the whipped cream to the cream cheese mixture, then add the melted white chocolate and mix until combined.

Divide the filling equally between 2 bowls, then mix about 75g [2¾oz] of the cherry mixture into one of the bowls.

cont...

Add about 1 Tbsp of the white cheesecake mixture into each semi-sphere mould, then add 1 tsp of the cherry mixture, then 1 Tbsp of the cherry cheesecake mixture and finish with another layer of white cheesecake mixture. Smooth the tops with a palette knife and freeze overnight.

To make the mirror glaze, soak the gelatine leaves in enough cold water to cover them. Set aside. Place the chocolate chips in a heatproof bowl and set aside.

Heat the liquid glucose, sugar and the 70ml [4½ Tbsp] water in a small saucepan over a low heat and stir until the sugar has dissolved. Increase the heat and boil until it reaches 104°C [219°F] on a sugar thermometer. Remove from the heat and add the condensed milk and enough food colour to achieve a deep red.

Squeeze the water from the gelatine leaves, add them to the sugar mixture and stir until completely dissolved. Pour the mixture over the white chocolate chips and stir until melted. Strain to remove any bubbles.

Unmould the cherry domes and place them on a wire rack with a tray underneath. Pour the mirror glaze generously over them, then sprinkle some coconut on top to imitate the warts typical of this mushroom. Refrigerate while you make the stalks.

To make the stalks, preheat the oven to 100°C fan [250°F/ Gas mark ½] and line a baking tray with baking paper.

Whisk the egg whites in a stand mixer or use a handheld electric whisk until frothy, then slowly add the caster sugar and whisk until stiff peaks form. Transfer the meringue to a piping [pastry] bag fitted with a plain nozzle. Pipe the stalks by piping a blob of meringue onto the tray then slowly pulling up so that the meringue tapers off. Bake for 1 hour.

Once the meringue stalks are ready, smooth the tops with a knife and place the cherry domes on top.

Slime Pudding

SERVES 6

400-g [14-oz] can condensed milk

400g [14oz] plain Greek yogurt

juice of 3 limes

juice of 2 lemons

leaf green food colour

yellow food colour

This is one of my favourite desserts and it just takes a few ingredients plus a little food colour. Keep tasting the mixture when adding the citrus juice so you can adjust to your taste. I like it rather tangy, so I add a lot of juice. It is so easy yet so effective as a dessert for a ghoulish dinner party.

Using a handheld electric whisk, mix the condensed milk and yogurt together in a large bowl. Mix the lime and lemon juices together, then slowly pour in enough for your taste. The mixture will thicken. Add some leaf green colour and a few drops of yellow to achieve a slimy hue. Cover the bowl with clingfilm [plastic wrap] and chill in the fridge for at least 3 hours, or ideally overnight.

Serve cold in 6 individual glasses or cauldrons.

Index

Acknowledgments

A huge thank you to everyone who made this book possible. First, my agent Vivienne Clore, who has excellent judgement when picking her clients! Céline Hughes and Nikki Ellis from Quadrille for embracing the 'dark' side of baking. Patricia Niven for the beautiful photography. Agathe Gits for the amazing props. Carole Hector and Sophie Garwood for their invaluable help in the kitchen.

To my family: my little witch in the making, Flora; my lunatic rescue wolfdog, Kato; and wonderful father to both, Will. Thank you to my friends for their constant support and to my fellow bakers for making my *Bake Off* experience an unforgettable one.

Publishing Director Sarah Lavelle
Senior Commissioning Editor Céline Hughes
Art Direction & Design Nikki Ellis
Photographer Patricia Niven
Food Stylists Helena Garcia, Carole Hector, Sophie Garwood
Prop Stylist Agathe Gits
Head of Production Stephen Lang
Production Controller Sinead Hering

Published in 2020 by Quadrille,
an imprint of Hardie Grant Publishing

Quadrille
52–54 Southwark Street
London SE1 1UN
quadrille.com

Text © Helena Garcia 2020
Compilation, design and layout © Quadrille 2020
Photography © Patricia Niven 2020

Cataloguing in Publication Data: a catalogue record for this book is available from the British Library.

ISBN 978 1 78713 600 7

Printed in China